SHAKESPEARE CELEBRATED

*Anniversary Lectures Delivered
at the Folger Library*

SHAKESPEARE
CELEBRATED

Anniversary Lectures Delivered

at the Folger Library

EDITED BY

Louis B. Wright

PUBLISHED FOR

The Folger Shakespeare Library

BY

CORNELL UNIVERSITY PRESS

Ithaca, New York

CORNELL UNIVERSITY PRESS

First published 1966

Library of Congress Catalog Card Number: 66-16738

PRINTED AND BOUND IN THE UNITED STATES OF AMERICA
BY VAIL-BALLOU PRESS, INC.

Preface

DURING 1964 many scholars visited the Folger Shakespeare Library to take part in the Four Hundredth Anniversary celebration of William Shakespeare's birth. Most of these scholars came to pursue their own research in problems concerned with Shakespeare's career, his reputation, or some aspect of his age. In the course of the year a number of visiting scholars gave lectures upon a variety of topics of interest to literary scholars and historians of the period. From among the lectures we have selected for publication seven that illustrate the range of subject matter covered by papers delivered during the anniversary year.

L. B. W.

June 15, 1965

Contents

SHAKESPEARE CELEBRATED

*Anniversary Lectures Delivered
at the Folger Library*

Shakespeare between
Two Civil Wars*

By C. V. WEDGWOOD

WHEN William Shakespeare was born, at Stratford-on-Avon in April, 1564, nearly eighty years had gone by since King Richard III had died on Bosworth Field and King Henry VII had united the Red Rose of Lancaster to the White Rose of York and inaugurated an epoch enriched

> with smooth-fac'd peace,
> With smiling plenty and fair prosperous days!

At least—as in the concluding words of Shakespeare's play on King Richard III—there was general lip service to this theme of the peaceful Tudor times which had made England whole again after the long and bloody civil wars between the rival dynasties of Lancaster and York.

As a picture of the times, this was of course something of

* Delivered March 2, 1964. Miss Wedgwood is the author of numerous books on English history and culture of the seventeenth century.

a simplification. England had not been lapped in unbroken peace and smiling plenty during the sixteenth century. On the contrary, the country had passed through the ravaging experience of the Reformation, with the economic upheaval and political risks involved. There had been numerous local uprisings, some, like the Pilgrimage of Grace, of considerable magnitude; there had been the attempt to set a rival sovereign, the prim, puritanical Lady Jane Grey, on the throne in place of Henry VIII's eldest daughter, the Catholic Mary Tudor; there had been, in the same cause, Sir Thomas Wyatt's ill-starred rebellion. There had been times when it looked—with the change of religion, with the ambitious intrigues of great families, with the uncertainty about the succession—as though there might be Wars of the Tudor Rose as bloody and as long as those of the White Rose and the Red. And all these political and religious tensions had been worked out in a country which was undergoing a prolonged social and economic crisis owing to the unprecedented increase in population and the decline in the value of money. Yet there had been no irretrievable descent into a divided government, and for this there was gratitude to the Tudors—to the cautious cunning of King Henry VII, to the tyrannical strength of Henry VIII; most of all, in the years during which Shakespeare grew up, to the wary skill of Queen Elizabeth and her great minister William Cecil.

It is obvious how much the shadow of past civil wars and the fear and horror of internecine conflict inspire the history plays of Shakespeare. The division of the country against itself is the ultimate disaster. So, in *King John,* the bastard Faulconbridge rallies the spirits of his countrymen in the face of French invasion:

This England never did, nor never shall,
Lie at the proud foot of a conqueror,
But when it first did help to wound itself. . . .
Come the three corners of the world in arms,
And we shall shock them. Nought shall make us rue,
If England to itself do rest but true.

To herself but true—it is the division of England that breeds danger. Shakespeare, in common with most of his contemporaries, thought with dread of that kind of war in which men of one nation and one speech, who should have been bound by ties of sacred loyalty to one sovereign, turned their swords upon each other:

The brother blindly shed the brother's blood,
The father rashly slaughtered his own son—

conflicts in which such a scene of tragedy could take place as that which Shakespeare depicts in *The Third Part of King Henry VI,* when the unfortunate King, left alone during the Battle of Towton, at first muses on the happiness that might have been his in a quiet and pastoral life and is interrupted by the entry of two soldiers, each triumphantly dragging a newly slain foe; only to discover, the one that he has killed his father, the other that he has killed his son. This scene, which epitomizes the horror of civil war, as Shakespeare and his contemporaries saw it, is not easy to act on the modern stage; it seems too improbable a coincidence; but it must be taken as a formal and tragic pageant of civil war: we have the King, unseen by the combatants, standing in the midst, hearing all that they say, feeling that as King he is the author of all these woes; and, symmetrically arranged one on either hand, the young man who uncovers the face of the man he has killed only to discover the features of his own father, and on the

C. V. Wedgwood

other side, a graybeard warrior who recognizes his victim too late as his own son. But this dramatic simplification is given a realist explanation: Shakespeare tells us just how it came about. The son says:

> From London by the King was I press'd forth;
> My father, being the Earl of Warwick's man,
> Came on the part of York, press'd by his master.

A factual statement—the boy, perhaps an apprentice in London, has marched with the London men under the King's banners; but the father is a tenant of the Earl of Warwick and so bound to serve in the wars as his overlord serves, against King Henry, with the Yorkist side—a straightforward explanation immediately understood by Shakespeare's audience, showing how, in the structure of their world and society, a young man who has done no more than follow a necessary obligation finds that he has become a parricide.

Shakespeare, following a fashion in praise and gratitude of the Queen and her forbears, loved to describe the England of his time in terms of pastoral tranquillity. Thus, in the play of Henry VIII, words of prophecy are spoken over the infant Elizabeth:

> She shall be lov'd and fear'd. Her own shall bless her:
> Her foes shake like a field of beaten corn,
> And hang their heads with sorrow. Good grows with her;
> In her days every man shall eat in safety
> Under his own vine what he plants, and sing
> The merry songs of peace to all his neighbors.

This emphasis on peace is paralleled by passages—many of them—on the horrors of war. There is the Bishop of Carlisle's famous prophecy in *Richard II* of ruin if the usurper Henry is made King:

4

And if you crown him, let me prophesy,
The blood of English shall manure the ground . . .
And in this seat of peace tumultuous wars
Shall kin with kin and kind with kind confound;
Disorder, horror, fear, and mutiny
Shall here inhabit, and this land be call'd
The field of Golgotha and dead men's skulls. . . .

Numerous other passages could be quoted from plays not necessarily about English history testifying to the intensity of Shakespeare's feeling on the horrors of war. Mark Antony prophesies over the dead body of Julius Caesar:

Domestic fury and fierce civil strife
Shall cumber all the parts of Italy;
Blood and destruction shall be so in use
And dreadful objects so familiar
That mothers shall but smile when they behold
Their infants quartered with the hands of war,
All pity choked with custom of fell deeds;
And Caesar's spirit, ranging for revenge,
With Até by his side, come hot from hell,
Shall in these confines with a monarch's voice
Cry "Havoc!" and let slip the dogs of war.

Where peace is concerned—or the peace of England, at any rate—does Shakespeare protest too much? In a way, yes, or at least the emphasis that he lays on the contrast between peace and war is essentially the emphasis of a man writing in an epoch when peace could not be regarded as the normal state of affairs; the order and tranquillity of society are something to be deeply thankful for, not something to be taken for granted.

England was, it is true, *internally* at peace, but from Shakespeare's twenty-fourth year until his fortieth, there was *external* war with Spain, and—as I need not remind you—there was a formidable threat of invasion in the year

5

of the Armada. In Scotland, the northern half of the same island, civil disorder seemed at times endemic, and there had been serious civil war in Shakespeare's youth. Just across the Narrow Seas, the Netherlands were the scene of fighting for almost the whole of Shakespeare's life, as the Dutch in a strenuous and painful struggle broke free of the Spanish yoke; and France was intermittently for many years plagued by an embittered and destructive war.

In the last act of *Henry V,* when after Agincourt the Duke of Burgundy plays the mediator between Henry V and the French king, Shakespeare puts into his mouth a plangent lament for peace, which has so long been absent from France, "this best garden of the world." All the fruits of the fertile land are destroyed:

> Her vine, the merry cheerer of the heart,
> Unpruned dies; her hedges even-pleached,
> Like prisoners wildly overgrown with hair,
> Put forth disorder'd twigs: her fallow leas,
> The darnel, hemlock, and rank fumitory
> Doth root upon, while that the coulter rusts
> That should deracinate such savagery.
> The even mead, that erst brought sweetly forth
> The freckled cowslip, burnet, and green clover,
> Wanting the scythe, all uncorrected, rank,
> Conceives by idleness and nothing teems
> But hateful docks, rough thistles, kecksies, burs,
> Losing both beauty and utility.
> And as our vineyards, fallows, meads, and hedges,
> Defective in their natures, grow to wildness,
> Even so our houses and ourselves and children
> Have lost, or do not learn for want of time,
> The sciences that should become our country.

This in the play is meant for the France of 1415; it could stand as well for the France of the 1590's before the strong

6

and healing hand of Henry of Navarre put an end to the divisions.

That such things had once been in England; that they still were in other less happy lands; that the threat of them was not altogether lifted but that by heaven's mercy and Elizabeth's skill they were held at bay; that they might come again: this is the unrestful political background of Shakespeare and his contemporaries.

And these things did come again in England: this is the meaning of my title, "Shakespeare between Two Civil Wars." Twenty-five years from Shakespeare's death the country was again to be split asunder by divided factions and divided interests, in a conflict the seeds of which were already sown in the reign of Queen Elizabeth I and had germinated fast under her successor, King James I. A conflict which, moreover, was to have its first pitched battle within a few miles, and almost within sight, of Shakespeare's home town of Stratford-on-Avon, just where the London road traverses the high escarpment of Edgehill. Here would be fought the first great battle between King Charles I and the forces of his Puritan Parliament. Along this road Shakespeare must often have traveled, must indeed sometimes have halted on that steep ridge on his way to London to look back over the fertile plain of Warwickshire; or on his journey home have greeted from here the familiar countryside of his childhood, looking across what is still one of the loveliest views in England. Here, soon after his death and in the lifetime of his daughter, Englishmen would fight Englishmen in deadly conflict.

The English Civil War, when it came, would be a war different in its causes and character from the dynastic feud which brought on the Wars of the Roses. It would have, indeed, more of the ideas that animate Shakespeare's Roman plays; conceptions of liberty and tyranny, of patrician and popular government, would be canvassed. Its avowed causes were the tension between Crown and Parliament and the mistaken efforts of the King to curb the Puritan movement, which had gone far beyond his, or anyone's, power to curb. Yet there would still be elements of the old feudal England in this later war of the seventeenth century. It would still have been possible—though I do not say that I have evidence of its actually occurring—that a young apprentice fighting for Parliament with the forces raised in London could have come face to face in battle with his father, a country gentleman whose loyalties had led him to follow the banners of some great landowner among the Cavaliers, maybe the Earl of Northampton from Compton Wynyates, who would be the greatest Cavalier landowner in Shakespeare's own region. There were certainly many examples of families divided against themselves in the civil wars of King Charles and his Parliament. We find the Countess of Denbigh, for instance, whose husband was slain on the King's side early in the war, writing to implore her son, who was in arms for Parliament, no longer to side with those who have been guilty of his father's blood. And there still survived into the Stuart epoch some of the picturesque accouterments of the Wars of the Roses—the standards carried before the troops were often gay with the heraldic devices of their leaders. There would be many on both sides, both for King and for Parliament, who felt, as their forbears had done in the Wars of the Roses, that they fought out of loyalty to the interest or influence of a particular family—for the Stanleys, and therefore for the King, in Lancashire; for the Fairfaxes, and therefore for Parliament, in Yorkshire— rather than for any deeper issues of politics or religion.

The differences between the profound constitutional conflict of the English seventeenth century and the dynastic strife of the fifteenth are greater than the similarities. But there were certain resemblances. If we think of Shakespeare's life in the perspective of time between these two civil conflicts, we see why peace was to him and to his contemporaries a precious thing, a delicate equilibrium threatened by dangers and instabilities in the state and marvelously maintained by the great Queen.

The dangers of war and disorder that seemed nearest to Shakespeare and his contemporaries were not, of course— for they had not the gift of prophecy—quite of the kind which ultimately broke upon the country. They feared, and justly feared, difficulties over the succession to the throne when Queen Elizabeth died. During Shakespeare's early years as a playwright and in his young maturity, in the 1590's, the Queen was old, childless, and extremely touchy when asked to make provision for the succession. Yet think what a disputed succession could have meant to England, a Protestant country with a considerable Catholic minority, in a period when Europe was divided by the Counter Reformation into two worlds, and when it would have been of inestimable value to Spain to have a friendly or even a satellite sovereign on the English throne. The dangers of Spanish invasion were not at an end with the defeat of the Armada in 1588. It was feared, and justifiably feared, that the death of Elizabeth might be the signal for disturbances in England—a disputed succession with the possibility of civil war and Spanish invasion.

C. V. Wedgwood

In fact, when the great Queen died on March 24, 1603, there was no trouble at all. Thanks to the forethought and skill of Robert Cecil, a minister devoted to the Queen but devoted also to the best interests of his country, King James VI of Scotland, Elizabeth's cousin, Mary Stuart's son, became King James I of Great Britain with a minimum of disturbance. Cecil had long been in correspondence with him, unknown to Elizabeth, carefully grooming and training him for the part of England's King.

Although we sometimes get the impression from popular textbooks that the Tudors were good and the Stuarts bad, and that King James was a sad falling-off after the great Elizabeth, this was not what was felt at the time. In 1603 the great majority of responsibly minded citizens welcomed the Scottish king with genuine enthusiasm. He was not the rather absurd figure that he later became but an intelligent man in the prime of life who had made a success of the difficult task of governing the self-willed and much divided nation of the Scots. He was a married man with a sprightly and fruitful wife, the Danish princess Anne, and a young family. His coming solved the nightmare succession problem which had hung over England pretty well ever since Henry divorced Queen Catherine of Aragon.

Now, it was the succession problem which had caused the Wars of the Roses: the dispute as to which of two branches of the royal house had the legal right to reign in England. The House of Stuart came in on a firm legitimate right—no doubtful marriages, no children of the left hand, but a straight descent from King Henry VII; and, unlike any sovereign of England for nearly a hundred years, King James already had two sons. Is it a wonder that the people

of England breathed more freely and poets were lavish of
praise to "our fruitful sovereign James"? To quote only
one of the many poems of welcome:

> Lo, here the glory of a greater day
> Than England ever heretofore could see
> In all her days! When she did most display
> The ensigns of her power, or whenas she
> Did spread herself the most, and the most did sway
> Her state abroad, yet could she never be
> Thus blest at home, nor ever come to grow
> To be entire in her full orb till now.

This refers of course to the union with Scotland; the poet
then goes on to praise the King:

> Glory of Men—this hast thou brought to us,
> And yet hast brought us *more* than this by far;
> Religion comes with thee, peace, righteousness,
> Judgment and justice which more glorious are
> Than all thy Kingdoms; and art more by this,
> Than Lord and Sovereign, more than Emperor,
> Over the hearts of men that let thee in
> To more than all the powers on earth can win.

Those lines, I need hardly add, are not by Shakespeare.
They are by Samuel Daniel. Shakespeare took no part in
the rather excessive adulation showered on the new king
by a great number of his contemporaries. He was not, of
course, above including some fulsome compliments to
King James in his plays. At the conclusion of the play of
King Henry VIII, praises for King James are tacked on a
little awkwardly after Cranmer's long speech of prophecy
about the glories of Elizabeth's reign: like the phoenix,
Cranmer declares, the ashes of Queen Elizabeth will create
another sovereign:

> As great in admiration as herself;
> So shall she leave her blessedness to one, . . .

11

Who, from the sacred ashes of her honor,
Shall star-like rise, as great in fame as she was,
And so stand fix'd: peace, plenty, love, truth, terror,
That were the servants to this chosen infant,
Shall then be his, and like a vine grow to him:
Wherever the bright sun of heaven shall shine,
His honor and the greatness of his name
Shall be and make new nations: he shall flourish,
And, like a mountain cedar, reach his branches
To all the plains about him.

And in *Macbeth,* the scene between Macduff and young
Malcolm, the legitimate King of Scotland—in which Macduff persuades the young man to invade the country and
dethrone the usurper who has murdered his father—that
scene is full of courteous glances at King James. Thus Malcolm lists what he calls the "king-becoming graces":

As justice, verity, temperance, stableness,
Bounty, perseverance, mercy, lowliness,
Devotion, patience, courage, fortitude.

These are a group of virtues such as King James would
have thought the ornament of good kings. For, though in
his numerous and eloquent political writings James took
the view that kings were God's vicegerents on earth and
could not therefore be questioned by their subjects however badly they behaved, yet he also held that the king's
duties to God, if not to his people, required him to reign
virtuously and to exercise just such king-becoming graces
as Malcolm names—always allowing that when he speaks of
"lowliness" he means of course lowliness and humility before God and God alone, not any unkingly bowing to the
will of his subjects, and by "courage" the profounder
virtue of moral courage, not mere physical courage, in
which King James was notoriously deficient.

A further passage in the same scene refers to Malcolm's contemporary, the eleventh-century King of England, Edward the Confessor, with whom he has taken refuge. Edward, a gentle and holy king, is described curing his subjects of the illness known as the "evil" by the sanctity of his touch. This miraculous healing quality of the royal touch was supposed to be inherited by English kings, and King James, after he ascended the throne, was pleased to exercise it; it ministered to his sense of the holy and God-given nature of kingship. Shakespeare in a short passage, usually omitted in modern stage productions, refers explicitly to it.

This whole scene between Malcolm and Macduff (barring only that great tragic passage in which Macduff hears of the murder of his wife and children by bloody Macbeth) is apt to be boring to modern audiences: it refers to political issues and ideas that are no longer of any live interest to us. Yet it contains one line and a half which are not only most beautiful and moving at the point where they come in the play but are striking to any historian interested in the decline of the English monarchy after the coming of the Stuarts.

When the young Malcolm at length ceases to temporize and declares that he is indeed ready and willing to come back to Scotland and liberate the oppressed nation from the tyrant Macbeth, he says to Macduff:

> What I am truly
> Is thine and my poor country's to command.

Now the phrase "thine to command" was in the English of Shakespeare's time no more than a catch phrase, a very common signature to a polite letter, the equivalent of

"Yours sincerely" today. But Shakespeare's genius is sometimes most strikingly shown in a way he has of taking a
phrase, which is a mere commonplace of speech, familiar
to all, and, by the way he places it, giving it an extraordinary weight. In this case it is the spacing that does it:
"thine to command" becomes "thine *and my poor country's* to command." This is the King making his vow of
service to his people, and I have heard that line given so
that it brought tears to the eyes.

 King James had a very high conception of the duties of
the kingly office, although he also had a very high conception of his power; his son King Charles, who was to be the
unfortunate protagonist of the war between king and Parliament, also felt deeply about his duties. Both these
sovereigns would have agreed that they had under God a
sacred obligation to their people and therefore were in a
sense "their country's to command." But neither of these
two Stuarts, nor, to be sure, Queen Elizabeth I, nor for
that matter Shakespeare himself, would have thought of
this as meaning that the sovereign was *answerable* to the
people in a democratic or parliamentary sense. They conceived it their duty to do what *they* thought right for their
subjects, having a charge, from God and from no one else,
to govern them. And it is no doubt in this sense that
Shakespeare puts the words into young King Malcolm's
mouth: he will give his utmost—his life, if need be—to save
his poor country from Macbeth and rule it as a just and
virtuous monarch should.

 But there has to be much practical wisdom as well as
political theory in maintaining a monarchy such as that
which the Tudors maintained. The first Stuart king, in an
admittedly difficult political situation, was to show that in

many ways, some of them rather simple and obvious, he had not the necessary wisdom. He lacked that sixth sense of what his people were thinking that had never failed Elizabeth, even in her last difficult and troubled years.

In *Measure for Measure* occurs a short, significant passage which is also thought to be a polite compliment to King James. The Duke, in the first scene, has just made over his power to the regent Angelo and is about to leave Vienna. Angelo not unnaturally suggests that he escort the Duke out of the town with due honors and attendance. To which the Duke replies:

> Give me your hand.
> I'll privily away. I love the people
> But do not like to stage me to their eyes.
> Though it do well, I do not relish well
> Their loud applause and *aves* vehement;
> Nor do I think the man of safe discretion
> That does affect it.

This is a side reference to the new king's notorious aversion to crowds. King James had psychological excuses for this. No man who had been as often manhandled and kidnapped as poor King James had been by his turbulent Scottish subjects in his youth would have been willing to expose himself to crowds. But Shakespeare in this passage seems to be praising this attitude in the King. He will not be a demagogue; he will not "stage himself," that is, play the actor, before the people's eyes. But is this conduct altogether wise in a ruler and did Shakespeare think it so?

Now what Shakespeare did or did not think about politics is a subject which has given scope for wide speculation; and it is part of Shakespeare's universal genius that we can always find in him a line of thought which is akin to our own. And therefore I do not claim to be proving anything about Shakespeare's way of thinking, but if we look at his attitude to rulers and to people there are certainly indications that he knew and understood very well—as how should he not?—the sensitive balance that must be maintained between the successful ruler and his people. And he knew also that those who shrink from contact with the rude multitude are not, generally speaking, the most successful in maintaining law, order, and their own authority.

Take *Richard II*—this is a study of marvelous subtlety showing a king who lives in a world of his own elegant and intellectual conceptions. Faced with the ultimate crisis, he plays his defeated part with undefeated authority. He confronts the successful rebel Bolingbroke:

> We are amaz'd; and thus long have we stood
> To watch the fearful bending of thy knee,
> Because we thought ourself thy lawful king;
> And if we be, how dare thy joints forget
> To pay their awful duty to our presence?
> If we be not, show us the hand of God
> That hath dismiss'd us from our stewardship.

Later in the tragedy of the deposition scene, the broken, powerless, degraded Richard makes the victorious Bolingbroke and all his faction look like a gang of vulgar bandits. Inevitably—in the longer perspective of history—one is reminded of the equally dramatic performance put on by King Charles I at his trial in 1649. But Richard cannot regain his crown by words, any more than King Charles could. We know that, whatever his just right to the throne, Richard lacked one vital thing that Henry Bolingbroke had—the popular touch. It is again part of Shakespeare's extraordinary genius that he first plants in our minds the idea of Bolingbroke's attraction for the multitude by letting Richard, in his days of power, describe it with scornful derision. He and his favorites have been watching and mocking at Bolingbroke as he goes by:

> Ourself and Bushy, Bagot here, and Green
> Observ'd his courtship to the common people;
> How he did seem to dive into their hearts
> With humble and familiar courtesy;
> What reverence he did throw away on slaves,
> Wooing poor craftsmen with the craft of smiles. . . .
> Off goes his bonnet to an oyster wench;
> A brace of draymen bid God speed him well
> And had the tribute of his supple knee,
> With "Thanks, my countrymen, my loving friends."

The dramatic irony of this scene is that King Richard does not realize that he is laughing at the very quality in Bolingbroke that is—for him—no laughing matter. Bolingbroke will be carried to the throne of England in part at least on the plaudits of the people; and Richard, the mocking, refined, out-of-touch Richard, will be murdered at Pomfret Castle.

So also King Henry VI, who lives in his studies and his prayers, cannot establish the relationship with the people that comes easily to such a bluff, brave wencher as his rival, King Edward IV. It is not, in the case of poor King Henry VI, for lack of trying. The recent revival of interest in this sprawling early trilogy, the three parts of *King Henry VI*, has introduced us to many subtleties in what was once a much neglected group of plays; and in seeing recent productions of them I have come to regret that Shakespeare worked on this subject before he had reached the height of his powers. For in Henry VI himself there is a sketch for a figure potentially as tragic as that of Richard II—a king whose impulses are all toward virtue, unselfishness, piety, and compassion, who only wants to do his duty as a king but is temperamentally unfitted for his part. This is his tragedy—that he means so much better toward his country than any of his rivals; but he shrinks, first behind his uncle regent, the good Duke of Gloucester, under whom things do not go too badly, and then behind his wife, Margaret of Anjou—the most horrible female character in all Shakespeare, not excepting Lady Macbeth—and everything goes very badly. But always he is completely remote from his people and can only wring his hands over their misfortunes:

> Woe above woe! grief more than common grief!
> Oh, that my death would stay these ruthful deeds!
> Oh, pity, pity, gentle heaven, pity! . . .
> Was ever king so griev'd for subjects' woe?

Had Shakespeare drawn Henry VI with all the power of his maturity, the King would be one of his great tragic creations.

In King Henry V, on the other hand, Shakespeare gives a picture of a king who has the common touch to perfection. We may not nowadays feel quite that sympathy with King Henry's aggressive militarism that the Shakespearean audience felt, but here is a ruler who exerts authority, commands loyalty, and inspires devotion because he can speak to the very hearts of his subjects. The young man who in his wild youth had kept company with Jack Falstaff and knew the taverns and back streets of London grows into the king who on the night before Agincourt can walk from tent to tent speaking as a friend and equal with his men, and who can rouse them on the day of battle with that great speech which through overuse and over-recitation has come to sound rhetorical to us, but which is in essence a very simple message of unity and encouragement to men whose only hope in a tight place is to stand together and fight hard:

> We few, we happy few, we band of brothers;
> For he today that sheds his blood with me
> Shall be my brother. Be he ne'er so vile,
> This day shall gentle his condition;
> And gentlemen in England now abed
> Shall think themselves accurs'd they were not here,
> And hold their manhoods cheap whiles any speaks
> That fought with us upon Saint Crispin's day.

This is Shakespeare's idea of how Henry V would have spoken at Agincourt in 1415, but it is a speech which breathes the spirit of the Elizabethan age, when, in time of national peril, the sovereign, though a woman, showed herself among her people, claimed that she had the heart of a king and was also proud to describe herself as "mere English."

In many other plays, besides the English history plays, we find Shakespeare noticing the importance for the successful leader—in politics or war—to have an understanding of the people, to be able at least to command their love. Thus Claudius says irritably of Hamlet after the murder of Polonius:

> How dangerous is it that this man goes loose!
> Yet must not we put the strong law on him.
> He's loved of the distracted multitude.

This is Hamlet's danger to the King—that he has the love of the people, which Claudius has not.

In *Coriolanus*—well, nobody can say that Shakespeare gives a very sympathetic picture of the Roman populace in that play; but the uncompromising *unwillingness* of Coriolanus to make the slightest attempt to understand or to get into contact with them is the political cause of his downfall. The theme of this great play is human pride rather than politics, but we notice again Shakespeare's awareness of the necessity of contact between ruler and the ruled. (The two tribunes of the people, incidentally, are such very unattractive characters because one senses in them that they are exploiting the people for their own ambitions; the true feeling of human relationship between the two hostile parties in Rome—plebs and patricians—is indicated in the small but important part of the veteran general Cominius, a good and generous leader, and in the humorous old patrician Menenius, who can, in his own way, talk to and reason with the people.)

Again, in *Julius Caesar* the conspirators are determined to have Brutus of their number because he is beloved of the people. As Casca says:

> Oh, he sits high in all the people's hearts,
> And that which would appear offense in us,
> His countenance, like richest alchemy,
> Will change to virtue and to worthiness.

And so, after the murder of Caesar, Brutus does indeed establish his authority over the people, so much so that one of them, mistaking the whole purpose of the murder, cries out excitedly "Let him be Caesar!" And it is only because Mark Antony commands an even greater popularity and a more effectively emotional brand of oratory that he wins the fickle multitude back to his side.

I have strayed a long way from *Measure for Measure* and that flattering reference to King James, praising him for being a superior being who would not court popularity with the people by "staging himself" to their eyes in public appearances. If Shakespeare respected this attitude, he clearly did not, in ordinary terms of human affairs, think it a wise one. And it is ironic that in this play, *Measure for Measure*, where the good Duke is depicted stealing away privately and eschewing contact with the vulgar, he is really, it turns outs, only doing it to deceive everyone. For he comes creeping back in disguise for the very purpose of moving unknown among his people and seeing how they are governed and what their opinion is of their laws and their rulers. Well, I mustn't make too much of that, because it is after all simply a part of the story that Shakespeare was using and may not have very much significance.

Now to turn from Shakespeare's treatment of the ruler in his relation to the people, to the people themselves. It is sometimes said that Shakespeare shows a general contempt, if not dislike, of the common people; in this, of course, we must beware of assuming that Shakespeare's opinions were the same as those that he put into the mouths of his characters. But such lines as Coriolanus' withering contempt of popular political opinions:

> Hang 'em! They say!
> They'll sit by the fire and presume to know
> What's done i' the Capitol, . . .
> Who thrives and who declines.

This is not necessarily Shakespeare's own view of popular opinion. Admittedly he puts this kind of thing very often into the mouths of his characters, despising the quick, emotional changes of the giddy-pated multitude. Casca, in *Julius Caesar*, describes with withering contempt the

C. V. Wedgwood

"hooting of the rabblement" when Caesar refused the crown:

If the tag-rag people did not clap him and hiss him, according as he pleased and displeased them, as they use to do the players in the theater, I am no true man. . . . He said, if he had done or said anything amiss, he desired their worships to think it was his infirmity. Three or four wenches where I stood cried, "Alas, good soul!" and forgave him with all their hearts. But there's no heed to be taken of them. If Caesar had stabbed their mothers, they would have done no less.

But this is Casca speaking, a character for whose opinions and conduct we need feel no great respect. Yet it is certainly true that Shakespeare in his treatment of the people in a crowd is rarely, if ever, favorable. The crowd is at best fickle—as in *Julius Caesar,* hailing Brutus with enthusiasm and half an hour later cheering Mark Antony while Brutus and Cassius, in flight, ride "like madmen through the gates of Rome"—at worst murderous—as in the killing of Cinna the poet in *Julius Caesar*; or in the horrible hanging and beheading of their victims by the ferocious mob in Jack Cade's rebellion in *Henry VI.* These crowd scenes depicting the English populace in full revolt echo the mad, dangerous voice of a hungry out-of-hand multitude which, at moments of economic distress in the sixteenth century, was a deeply feared threat to Shakespeare's own world; and the voice of the dispossessed of Shakespeare's time, with their fear and hatred of enclosures that took away the common land, and their suspicion of lawyers and educated men, rings out in the words of the rebel leader Jack Cade: "All the realm shall be in common," he promises, "in Cheapside shall my palfrey go to grass. . . . There shall be no money: all shall eat and drink on my score." "Let's kill all the lawyers, the first thing we do,"

22

shouts one of his followers. They hang the town clerk of Chatham because he admits he can read and write; and when the captured Lord Say quotes a Latin tag in speaking to them, the rebel Cade cries: "Away with him! he speaks Latin. . . . Take him away and behead him."

These cries for the return of the common land, this animosity against lawyers and anger at any who dares to speak a language or use phrases not understood by the ordinary people, all these demands of Jack Cade's mob, would be heard again in the Civil War against King Charles after Shakespeare's death; this time not as mere brutish outcries, but respectably argued and developed and set down in pamphlets.

But if Shakespeare depicts the common people with no redeeming graces when we see them as a mob, he can and does show the individual man of the people with sympathy and admiration. Thus, in *King Lear,* in the horrifying scene of Gloucester's blinding by the unspeakable Cornwall and his wife Regan, it is one of the servants who protests at the action and is killed trying to prevent it, and the rest of the servants, after Cornwall and Regan have gone, do what they can to assist the blinded Gloucester. The soldiers, whose conversations on the night before Agincourt we listen to in *Henry V,* are intelligent men with ideas of their own; and the native generosity, good nature, and loyalty of simple people is depicted in such characters as the old shepherd in *The Winter's Tale,* Adam in *As You Like It,* the groom who visits King Richard II at Pomfret Castle, and others. In *Love's Labor's Lost,* it is the ordinary man, Costard, whose unfailing good sense, good humor, and plain speaking is used as a foil to the attitudinizing of the King and his bright young noblemen. No one would pretend that Shakespeare idealizes or makes a hero of the Common Man, a thing completely outside the conceptions of his epoch or the taste of his audiences, but his treatment of such characters, though it is best known in the uproarious comedy of *A Midsummer Night's Dream,* is by no means always comic but can be serious and sympathetic. And one cannot conceive of Shakespeare taking the view that fine actions and feelings are the prerogative of the nobly born, as, for instance, the French poet Pierre Corneille argued with all solemnity; in one of his later plays, *Heraclite,* the historic incident which he has dramatized turns on the self-sacrifice of a servant, a nurse, who saves the life of the Emperor's child in a palace revolution. Such an action, Corneille explains, cannot in a seemly heroic drama be performed by someone so low in the social scale; he changes the nurse into a lady of noble birth. It is inconceivable that Shakespeare should have done such a thing. He was too great a realist for that. If his mobs are silly and brutal, it is because the crowd—as a crowd—is both these things. But the individual man, whatever his social status, is treated with the respect he merits.

It should have appeared when King James ascended the throne of England in peace, and when he speedily made peace abroad and ended the war with Spain, that an age of settled tranquillity was at hand. The King's favorite motto was "Blessed are the peacemakers," and his intention was to secure peace abroad by a discreet balance of alliances and to maintain order at home by the power and authority of the Crown. It was an admirable ideal, but the King failed to reckon with the complex forces at work in his new country. The inadequate revenues of the Crown, the consequent coercive power that Parliament had over the mon-

archy: this was one problem. The spread of Calvinism—
Puritanism in its Calvinist form, that is—among his subjects, and the consequent resistance to royal power where
it was felt to be at variance with the word of God: this was
another problem. The failure to solve either of these problems, and worse, the positive exacerbation of both of them
by the policies of James and of his son Charles, led in the
end to civil war. The situation was never easy, but the in-
capacity of either of these kings to understand or to react
to public opinion was undoubtedly an element in hasten-
ing on the crisis of civil war.

Shakespeare died in 1616 and wrote his last play some
years before that; he did not therefore live to see the situation reach the most critical stage. Yet a man so sensitive to
human values and relationships must have felt already
some uneasiness. He knew that King James shunned public appearances and did not care to show himself to the
people, for he had commented on this with superficial
approbation, or at least in terms of compliment, in *Measure for Measure*. But, as a practical observer of human
affairs, we know from many other indications that Shakespeare both fully understood and valued the practice of a
ruler who responds more freely to the people and has the
art of pleasing them—an art not gained by keeping at a distance, an art brilliantly practiced, and with no loss of dig-
nity, by the wise and wary old Queen. It was a foreign
observer, a Venetian envoy, who noticed in the reign of
King James that the English, who when he first ascended
the throne had been such worshipers of royalty that they
would go any distance to see their sovereign pass by, did
not a few years later show any particular interest in his
rather infrequent public appearances. After the adulation

which had been showered on the King at his first arrival, the prestige and popularity of the Crown fell gradually, and then with increasing rapidity, into a decline.

It would be an idle exercise to seek for any barometer of King James's popularity in the strength of the monarchy in the middle and later plays of Shakespeare. In his full maturity he is dealing with matters more eternal than the passing politics of England—with the storms and problems of the human soul—but when politics are a part of his theme, the clear beliefs which guided him in his earlier history plays seem to have given place to a more clouded and obscure attitude. The early history plays—the sequence which tells the story of Richard's deposition, the troubled reign of Henry IV, the victories of Henry V, the long wars under Henry VI, culminating in the murderous reign and death of Richard III—these are dominated by the idea of the king's sacred right. Richard II was a bad king, but he was the legal one. Henry IV is a usurper, and his issue (in spite of the glorious Henry V) are accursed with wars and troubles, until calm is restored by the return of the crown to its true place once again. This theme of legitimacy can even be traced out in the play of *King John,* where Shakespeare accepts the murdered child Arthur, John's nephew, as the rightful King, in touching lines:

> The inheritance of this poor child,
> His little kingdom of a forced grave.
> That blood which ow'd the breadth of all this isle,
> Three foot of it doth hold.

And again, when they carry away the little boy's dead body:

26

How easy dost thou take all England up!
From forth this morsel of dead royalty,
The life, the right, the truth of all this realm
Is fled to heaven.

Order in the state depends on the sacred authority of the Crown, passed down in due right of succession; deviation spells disaster, divided loyalties, disorder, and civil war.

In his earlier years, Shakespeare seems to accept this idea with consistency. But already, in *Hamlet,* a play which presents, among so many other facets, a complex study in politics, there are puzzling things. It contains, for instance, one of Shakespeare's most firmly phrased and most assured statements about the sanctity of kingship:

There's such divinity doth hedge a king
That treason can but peep to what it would,
Acts little of his will.

But who is it who thus boldly claims to be protected by his Divine Right? It is Claudius, King of Denmark, a usurper, a murderer, and an adulterer. And Claudius *knows* that he is all these things; and the audience also knows it. The words are not out of character in the context; he is a bold man, bluffing out a difficult situation, quelling the armed and furious Laertes. But at a period when the sanctity of the monarch was a serious doctrine, and one to which Shakespeare himself apparently subscribed, to put it into the mouth of a king so unsanctified as Claudius gives it an ironic edge.

In the Roman plays, though he is more concerned with character than politics, Shakespeare explores the reasons for the breakdown of a society with a cooler realism than he does in the English history plays and with perhaps some glances at contemporary political theory of the popular rather than the monarchical kind, part classical, part forged on the anvil of the French religious wars.

> My soul aches [says Coriolanus]
> To know, when two authorities are up,
> Neither supreme, how soon confusion
> May enter 'twixt the gap of both and take
> The one by the other.

The danger of two nearly equal factions had been seen in the French religious wars; it would come soon in England in the deadlock between the power of the King and that of Parliament. In the same play the plebeian party claims that the city—Rome—*is* the people; that is, the state *is* the people, and the magistrates rule only by their consent—a doctrine already common in France in the civil wars, which would become a dominating theory in the English Civil War.

When we come to *Julius Caesar* and *Antony and Cleopatra*, if one thinks of the intensity of Shakespeare's earlier insistence on the blessings of peace and order, one is surprised to find that the character who should represent that element in the state of Rome, namely, Octavius Augustus, is treated with so little sympathy and respect by Shakespeare. He is introduced to us first in the scene in which Antony, Lepidus, and he are settling who shall be proscribed. His first words suggest a repellent character:

> Your brother too must die; consent you, Lepidus?

And although in *Antony and Cleopatra* he is given the opportunity to speak, rather drily, of the peace and order which he hopes the Roman world may in the end enjoy, the sympathies of the spectator are not at any moment enlisted toward this desirable end but are wholly drawn toward those two fascinating irresponsibles, Cleopatra and Mark Antony.

What does this mean? Well, probably nothing except that the mature Shakespeare found the exploration of character, with its mixture of weakness, courage, selfishness, self-sacrifice, love, folly, and calculation, more interesting by far than the politics of the Roman empire.

Whatever the faults of King James's government as King of Great Britain, his court was a generous patron of the theater, and Shakespeare enjoyed fame, prosperity, and continuous court patronage, his plays being put on for every festival occasion. At the wedding of the King's daughter, the beautiful Princess Elizabeth, to a German prince, the Elector Palatine, Shakespeare's *Tempest* was only one out of several of his plays which graced the festivities—though the most suitable, with its tale of love and magic and a princely betrothal. The masque shown by Prospero to Miranda and her Ferdinand, with its promise of peace and fruitfulness, was perhaps written in for the occasion. It was only partly successful as prophecy—theirs was indeed a happy and fruitful marriage—thirteen children—but Princess Elizabeth and her husband by inept policy triggered off the Thirty Years' War in Germany, lost all their lands, and spent most of their lives in poverty-stricken exile.

At the time of the wedding rejoicings, Prince Charles, the future Charles I, was twelve years old. He grew up to be an enthusiastic patron of the arts and the theater, and at his court—Shakespeare being nine years dead when he came to the throne—Shakespeare's plays were often given, indiscriminately mixed with lesser works by a new generation of dramatists—Carlell, Shirley, Davenant—as well as the securely established Ben Jonson and John Fletcher. The King's taste was for the poetic, the lyrical, the baroque. It is recorded that a performance of *Cymbeline* was greatly enjoyed by him.

The cautious suspicion of the populace felt by King James hardened in his son Charles into something like real dislike. "He hates the people," the observant Venetian agent reported in his dispatches. Worse, like some kings whom Shakespeare had depicted, he had no respect for their opinions and no sense of his mounting danger. And so it would happpen that under his rule the English would no longer be "singing the merry songs of peace to all their neighbors," but on the green slope of Edgehill in Shakespeare's country, a few miles only from the church where his bones lay and where "a neat bust of that famous poet Mr. William Shakespeare" was already a tourist attraction, his countrymen would stand arrayed in battle opposite each other, and in the afternoon sunlight of an October day in 1642 would "cry 'Havoc!' and let slip the dogs of war."

The Road to Jamestown *

By DAVID B. QUINN

THE road to Jamestown is a route which could be traced chronologically as, voyage after voyage, the English learnt a little and forgot a little about Atlantic voyaging and about the lands that lay to the west in Western European latitudes. But it is also a story which can be broken down analytically, topic by topic. I am going to try to combine the two methods—to pick out and discuss one topic, the term "colony" and the meanings and implications of it for the English, and then I will say a little about the foundation of the Jamestown settlement in 1606–1607.

Shakespeare's life almost exactly spanned the period when the settlement of North America was transformed from a concept into reality. On April 23, 1564, when Shakespeare is believed to have been born, there was not a single European settlement north of Mexico. In 1616,

* Delivered May 7, 1964. Mr. Quinn is Andrew Geddes and John Rankin Professor of Modern History at the University of Liverpool.

when he died, there were no less than six centers of European settlement, all small, but some with a great potential: St. Augustine, Jamestown, Bermuda, Port Royal, Quebec, the Avalon Peninsula in Newfoundland. One was Spanish, two were French, three English. Bermuda was reasonably well isolated; repeated efforts did not make Newfoundland more than a potential colony. Jamestown, alone of the English settlements at that time, seemed to have the likelihood of a great future. Jamestown was the first enduring English colony in the West. How it came to be so is partly the result of the effort poured into it from 1606 onward; but it is partly also the result of the trial-and-error approach to American colonization which gives me my theme.

What a colony is, is not so easily defined as might be thought. It involves, of course, bringing people from their homeland to a new territory to remain for some time, if not in perpetuity. It requires an appreciable quantity of equipment for them to be sent from their home. It involves, almost certainly, a degree of assistance to them until they can become self-supporting. A colony has in it at least the seeds of permanence. Yet once we go beyond these simplest definitions it becomes difficult to draw a clear line between temporary and permanent settlements. Some settlements were temporary enough yet regular; some systematic settlements proved by miscalculation or accident to be quite temporary. In studying the earliest beginnings of settlement we should take nothing for granted: each kind of contact, the details of each phase, have a certain significance.

From shortly after 1500 (if not before) fishing vessels

from west European ports, from Lisbon in the south (lat. 39° N.) to Bristol in the north (lat. 52° N.), were going each year to a sharply defined area off the American coast, namely, to the Grand Banks off Newfoundland and to the shorelines of Newfoundland and Cape Breton Island. Besides fishing from their boats for cod, these ships put into the same harbors each year, traded goods with other vessels there, ferried freshly caught fish ashore to parties of men who salted and air-dried them on land in a rather long-drawn-out process, and often had some social meetings in harbor or even on land with their fellow seamen before leaving for Europe between August and November.

By the mid-sixteenth century there were over one hundred ships going each year to the fisheries; by 1585 as many as two hundred, manned by men who were subjects of the rulers of Portugal, Spain, France, England, or Ireland; by 1620 probably some five hundred. The phrase "summer settlement" well describes these maritime activities on Newfoundland and adjoining shores. It may be that a few tough men were left from time to time over the hard winter in the huts which held gear and boats, to guard them against pilfering Indians or marauding early comers of the next season, but no proof of this has yet been found. The fisheries were more nearly colonies than we sometimes care to admit; but, in spite of the regularity with which ships and men crossed the Atlantic to them, and the familiarity with which they treated American land, they were not permanent settlements; they lacked the social and physical continuity out of which stable organizations on land could grow. And it is perhaps significant that in the seventeenth century the fishermen were often foes rather than friends of the people who attempted to live all the year round in Newfoundland: they recognized a basic difference in their status.

Or what about the whale fishermen? The Basques had been well out into the Atlantic after whale in the fourteenth century. Basque speakers, whether technically of Spanish or French nationality, were early on the coasts of eastern North America, chasing especially the true (or right) whale, and, when they penetrated the Gulf of St. Lawrence, as they seem to have done early in the sixteenth century, the white whale (or beluga) as well. They, like the Arctic and Antarctic whalers of sailing days in the nineteenth century, did not necessarily reckon to complete a voyage in a single season. Whalebone, spermaceti, and oil, when properly cared for, would keep for a long time, and so two-year voyages became not uncommon, perhaps with relief ships being sent out from the home ports to help tide the whalers over the second season. The harbors or shore camps where these tough, expert teams wintered were probably mainly in western Newfoundland or on Anticosti. By remaining over the winter, such crews established a continuity which was lacking in the codfishery. They were, perhaps, a shade more nearly a colony. Yet they did not create any substantial shore establishment or a year-round population. And it is not yet known whether wintering was normal, rather than abnormal, or that it was always done by a particular ship and crew at the same place.

The fisheries, whether for cod or whale, were wholly external to America. But when we come to furs we have a commodity the harvesting of which could be done only in association with the aboriginal Americans (if so we may call the Indians and Eskimos). Fur trading was done by Basque and French fishermen around Cape Breton Island and in the Gulf of St. Lawrence with Micmac and Montagnais Indians who came down to the shores for their summer fishing and collecting. To begin with, it remained a sideline to the cod harvest, but it turned the traders' attention to the land, to the people, to the need, in places, for temporary shore camps where exchanges could take place. Trade of any sort involved finding out what the Indians needed or coveted; it brought businessmen into some commercial involvement with the first American market.

Cartier discovered in 1534 how Indians from the interior, drawn from Iroquois and Algonkian cultures alike, came down as far as the Gaspé Peninsula to fish and to exchange furs and copper for fish amongst each other. Later, when he wintered near Quebec in 1535–1536, he found that the best center for a trading base was at Tadoussac, at the mouth of the Saguenay, a traditional Indian summer meeting place. It now seems certain that by 1580, or shortly after, individual Breton, Norman, French Basque, and Spanish Basque vessels were going there each summer for furs. The "summer settlement" of the fisheries was translated firmly to dry land, as the fur trade was established on the St. Lawrence and became a slight step nearer to the colony in giving the traders an additional stake in the land, without impelling them at once toward the continuity of a year-round settlement.

The round-the-year trading station was one step further on. It may be that the Bristol merchants, who, in association with a few Portuguese, were trading across the Atlantic between 1501 and 1506, attempted to establish some sort of trading post (possibly in New England; conceivably in Newfoundland). We have indications in the stores taken out that this may have been so but not enough knowledge of what went on to be sure if an English party actually spent a winter in the West. Cartier's winter camp near Quebec in 1535–1536 was partly an experiment in maintaining such a post to tap the St. Lawrence fur trade at what was thought to be the upper limit of navigation for ocean-going vessels. The cold and the heavy mortality over the winter made him break the continuity he may have intended. There could, indeed, have been other small experiments of this sort of which we know nothing. We know that, more than a generation later (in 1583), Etienne Bellenger of Rouen set out with the intention of staying at such a fur-trading post on the shores of what are now Nova Scotia and New Brunswick, though he sailed home without doing so, probably because of an Indian attack in which he lost some men and the pinnace intended for the use of the settlement. The incentive to found a trading post was an expression of the trend toward monopoly in a growingly valuable business, once beaver came to be in great demand for hats in France. The possessors of an overwinter post could catch the earliest furs the Indians could be induced to bring, could exclude strange ships from the harbor or river, could harry interlopers who got on shore so that the whole of the available fur supply over a considerable area could be tapped by a single syndicate. At Tadoussac in 1600 a Breton-Norman group of businessmen put a few traders ashore for the winter to try out a new type of trading post, but the resulting casualties were so great that the survivors came home in 1601. The extension of the summer trading settlement into the year-round trading post was seen to be impracticable on a small-scale basis.

The English had to learn this too, though their experience was not so hard. Bartholomew Gosnold proposed in 1602 to leave a dozen men in a little fortlike trading post he had built in Cuttyhunk so that the furs which the Wampanoag and Narragansett Indians could collect should be acquired ready for shipment the following summer in 1603. But when the "Concord" was about to leave, the men became panic-stricken. They were afraid of the Indians. They insisted on being brought home. Such a small, purely commercial post was, indeed, very doubtfully viable. Instead, in 1603, when Martin Pring came to trade in Cape Cod Bay, he contented himself with making a strong trading enclosure on land, which provided him with a three months' summer settlement at which Indians, bringing furs for sale, could be received and recompensed and which he abandoned once the season was over.

These small projected or attempted trading posts were still focused on Europe rather than on America. They were a potential convenience in the operation of a branch of commerce which was becoming of some importance. Because they did involve year-round settlement, the appropriation of at least a small amount of land, and close relations, if only for short periods, with the Indians, the year-round trading posts represent an appreciable step, almost a jump, from the type of contact represented by the fishing and whaling operations. But their scale was necessarily so small, their functions inevitably so narrow, that, as so conceived, they had little potentiality.

Once we leave the simplest project for a trading post

concerned with the provision of a permanent exchange point for a commodity such as furs, we are faced with a multifaceted situation: to treat this chronologically would involve confusion and repetition. We can, however, segregate particular elements in the colonizing process which led toward continuous community settlement.

We can, I think, credit the French and the English with an experimental attitude toward the New World which is scarcely seen amongst the Spaniards or Portuguese, who seem to us to press on toward their ends of commercial or religious exploitation with little reflection or pause to study the social and physical terrain into which they are advancing. *Their* reflections are by way of afterthoughts, often regrets at how much they have undone in their precipitate and egotistic progress. We get the new proto-scientific spirit in Verrazzano, a detached and critical view of the North American coast and its inhabitants. We get more of it in French Florida, where Jacques Le Moyne is sent out to study and draw and paint what he saw of both Indian life and the natural products of the area. The French Florida colony of 1564–1565 was not designed as an experimental laboratory for the study of aboriginal America, but it had the elements of one consciously embedded in it. More deliberately scientific was the Roanoke colony of 1585–1586. There Thomas Hariot, a brilliant young mathematical theorist with a practical bent toward astronomy and navigation, was persuaded to divert his interests to the learning of the Indian language of the region, studying the Indians, preparing and executing a thorough natural history and cartographical survey. And in association with him went the artist John White, recording in sharply naturalistic sketches the appearance of the subjects with which Hariot's survey was concerned. We have enough of their combined work left (though far from all of it) to see that the colony of 1585–1586 was in a real sense a laboratory. It was also a site where experiments could be made with the growing of plants, whether from seeds brought from England or plants brought from the West Indies or culled from local sources. Here the intention was better than the performance, but a beginning at least was made in penetrating the secrets of American ecology. The Roanoke colony was essentially provisional and temporary. Not waiting to be transformed into a community, the men returned with Drake in 1586 but left something new, the beginning of the assembly of an objective body of knowledge, essential if systematic colonization was to be embarked on. Champlain's expeditions had always something of this synthesizing character: mapping, listing, and describing; drawing as well as narrating. So, too, did the Waymouth voyage to Maine in 1605 through the work of its narrator, James Rosier. Rosier, who appears as another Hariot (though he has left us still less to judge him by), and the Indians brought back from Maine provided Sir John Popham and Sir Ferdinando Gorges with a view of New England which influenced a whole generation's activity there.

Mineral extraction might most easily have led to permanent settlement on North American shores had any sufficiently rich sources been found close to the coast. Nothing else would have led so quickly to the mobilization of enough capital and human enthusiasm (and greed) to plant men firmly at an early stage in North American soil. But American gold remained a will-o'-the-wisp, often hinted at, sometimes thought to be found, twice only, in the sixteenth century, causing something of a gold rush. The first such rush was when Cartier found gold and precious stones, as he thought, on the shores of the St. Lawrence in 1542; but he had no sooner got them to France than all were found to be worthless. The second was when Frobisher collected some metamorphic rock on Baffin Island in 1576, was given a mistaken assay when he returned to England, and brought out a fleet to extract minerals galore in 1577. The rock was metalliferous (micaceous, at least) but not capable of returning precious metals; yet sufficiently optimistic refining reports were made to lead to the preparation of a permanent mining camp in 1578. The working-out of lists of equipment for one hundred men for the cold northern winter, and, above all, the construction of a large prefabricated building as their main residence, was an important exercise in settlement logistics. In the event, the ship containing half the building did not arrive; the settlers used this as an excuse for refusing to stay. The ships when they returned were met with the news that no gold could in fact be extracted, so that the mining camp, if established, might very well have been left to its fate. This solitary experiment exercised some influence: it set certain men thinking of how, precisely, a settlement was to be equipped. The gold lure, too, was to be one attraction, a fitful one it is true, which held men's attention to America and even played its part in the survival of Jamestown in 1607.

Fishery control and protection was an incentive to the establishment of a naval and fiscal outpost which might provide a center round which settlement could grow. The fishing on the Newfoundland Banks brought, as we saw, first scores and later hundreds of ships into the many harbors which pierced that jagged island. Requiring ground on which to dry their fish, most of the fishermen had a stake in the land, if not a permanent one. They established the tradition of first come, first served in the drying stages at each port. What quarrels there were, were settled by the port admiral, the captain or master of the first vessel to put in. As the custom of leaving behind some of the boats used in the fishery became prevalent, quarrels over stealing became more difficult to avoid. Further, the fishery became vulnerable to pirates, and, as the Anglo-Spanish friction verged toward war, there were attempts by English privateers to destroy the Iberian elements in the fishery.

Sir Humphrey Gilbert sailed into St. John's Harbor in August, 1583, determined to coerce the fishermen into acknowledging him as their overlord, submitting to English laws forbidding the exercise of Catholic religious ceremonies on land, and laying the ground for the acknowledgment of Elizabeth I as Queen. By a show of force he managed to get the vessels in the harbor to purchase passports to fish and to pay him (in kind) for the future lease of drying grounds on shore. This was excellent in theory, but Gilbert sailed away (to his death) leaving no one to enforce his control. It seems that his brother, Sir John Gilbert, made a half-hearted attempt to implement his regulations in 1584, which he later gave up as impracticable. Yet Edward Hayes in 1586 drew up the most elaborate scheme for the control of the fishery. If some royal finance might be found to supplement private investment and a man of sufficient authority be induced to head the local government, a garrison with a naval patrol might lead on to a rich and prosperous settlement battening on the fishermen. This never came to pass, but it remained an element in the attitude of projectors toward Newfoundland and of fishermen resisting the notion of any control or even the existence of shore settlers, and it was influential later in the experiments and controversies in New England over the possible links between fishery regulation and settlement in the 1620's.

One simple attraction of the colonial field was in providing a dumping ground for criminals. Sixteenth-century England was cruel even to its minor offenders and strung up many of them with little compunction, but it was not a slave society and from time to time the idea of getting rid of its offenders by shipment to the West appeared. It could seem a simple matter of social convenience, but it might also be made to seem a humanitarian measure. To the younger Richard Hakluyt in 1584, for example, it seemed a social waste to have so many people, many of them in his eyes socially estimable, lying in jail for debt or for very minor offenses. Why not release them out of the country and put them to socially useful work by making them colonists? There was, further, the strongest feeling in Tudor England that if you were able to work and did not work you were a criminal and ought to be treated as such. Society there was in sufficient flux to have much unemployment, both casual and long-term alike. The state would take no direct responsibility for the unemployed man. He must be harried into finding work somehow, or be crowded into slavelike workhouses, or beaten until he asserted his energies by finding work. In 1598 he could, by act of Parliament, be banished to any part of the world to which officials might like to consign him. In the first set of detailed orders under this act which have survived (in September, 1603), Newfoundland (here probably meaning any part of North America) is mentioned as one intended dumping ground.

The convict disposal problem was not regarded in a purely negative sense. Convict labor was the easiest to direct. Soldiers might be sent to colonize under orders, but there were menial construction jobs to which they would not turn their hands: convicts could be made to do the dirty work of building an overseas settlement. As early as 1498 Cabot was said to be taking convicts with him to help build a way station on the route to Asia. Frobisher apparently did take some with him to his mining camp on Baffin Island in 1578, though he did not leave them behind. Edward Hayes in 1586 asked to be allowed to export criminals as galley slaves for the coastal patrol he wished to establish at the Newfoundland fishery. In 1598 a convict group was very nearly sent to work a fishery on the Magdalen Islands in the Gulf of St. Lawrence. In the Virginia colony transportees formed, from almost the earliest stages in its formation, one significant source of labor. But the convict was, when used in this way, always an artifact in colonial pioneering, not a thinking, constructive force within it.

The able-bodied beggar was seen as a social dissentient liable, if allowed to sin against the state by not working, to harbor thoughts of disrupting the social order. The religious dissentient was a new phenomenon with which all post-Reformation European states had to deal. Brutal as Elizabethan England could be, there was an undoubted reluctance to massacre those Englishmen on the Catholic Right or the Ultra-Protestant Left who failed to fit themselves within the ecclesiastical structure designed by Elizabeth and her parliaments. (This reluctance to kill heretics

in the mass was not shared by Catholic Spain or by Ultra-
montane Catholics across the Channel.) At the same time
it was clear that Catholics who did not come to church
must be treated with some marks of social disapproval and
subjected to some degree of coercion: after the papal bull
of 1570 they tended more and more to be treated as posi-
tively criminal. At the same time, Presbyterian elements in
the established church were busy trying to alter it in ways
which seemed almost equally culpable and punishable.
When Protestants went further and broke from the church
entirely, forming sects of their own, it seemed clear that
fire and sword might be used to coerce them, though the
separatist congregations who were declared punishable by
the act of 1593 contributed no more than a handful of
martyrs to the Establishment.

As in the case of ordinary convicts, America seemed a
possible repository for dissentient religious elements where
they might be allowed to run almost free. We have sugges-
tions as early as 1573 for exporting Presbyterians, though
to Ireland not to America: Hakluyt urged in 1584 that
Presbyterian clergy be sent to preach to the American Indians instead of disrupting the calm of Anglican ortho-
doxy. At the same time, as information began to be spread
about the potentialities of North America by Richard
Hakluyt and others, America came to seem to some of the
oppressed dissenters a new and potentially attractive home
across the Atlantic.

In 1582 many well-connected and well-endowed Catholic gentlemen were attracted by a land speculation project
put out by Sir Humphrey Gilbert. Inspired by him and
helped by the Secretary of State, Sir Francis Walsingham,
they proposed to shift whole social units, consisting of Eng-

lish Catholics who were being bled by discriminatory taxation and other kinds of pressure, to eastern North America. Sir Thomas Gerrard of Lancashire and Sir George Peckham of Buckinghamshire were the leaders. Between them they parceled out millions of acres at Verrazzano's "Refugio" on what we now know as Narrangansett Bay. In point of fact, not one of them set foot there. Some were scared away by the Spaniards who threatened to come and cut their throats, some by the English refugees on the Continent who warned them that they were running away when they should be building up the Catholic community for the overthrow of the Queen, others still by the failure and death of Sir Humphrey Gilbert, who had gone out in 1583 to make a reconnaissance of his new territories. Peckham tried unsuccessfully to keep the plan going but gave up in 1584. The notion survived, however. When James I came to the throne it looked as if the situation of the Catholics might become easier, but, disappointed by not getting toleration, a number of them decided to see whether the shores of eastern North America, between Chesapeake Bay and the newly discovered Cape Cod, might not provide some such refuge as they had formerly sought. George Waymouth, in fact, led the reconnaissance expedition too far north and explored only the St. George's River and a few offshore islands in Maine. When he returned, Lord Arundell of Wardour had got tired of the idea—the Catholic refugees on the Continent still proving hostile—and went soldiering in the Spanish Netherlands for a time. Then the Gunpowder Plot killed Catholic initiative and the Catholics drew back.

But land alone, without a religious incentive, could be a sufficient objective to spur men to plan colonies. Gilbert

45

got in Ireland a strong sense that the greatest spur to younger sons like himself was the prospect of that landed power and authority from which they were normally debarred by the rules of primogeniture in England. In 1582–1583, besides inciting Catholic gentry to leave England, he planned a fantastic feudal lordship for himself and his friends, located, we presume, near the Catholic center on Narragansett Bay, though perhaps to the south and west of it, conceivably at Verrazzano's Angoulême (the Hudson basin). As Lord Paramount he would live in scarcely subregal state, commanding armies and navies, dominating councils, parliaments, and law courts, having below him a long hierarchy of dependents and sub-dependents. If this remained a paper scheme only, it was nevertheless an ideal which hung before the eyes, for example, of Sir Ferdinando Gorges, who for forty years tried under various devices to bring it into effect in New England. It was an element too in getting so many landowners, especially M.P.'s to invest substantially in the Virginia Company, since, when the lands were shared out eventually, they hoped to find themselves better off territorially than they would have been in England with a similar expenditure. And, indeed, in the longer run a few of them were. It is not easy, either, to decide whether it was their desire for Catholic separatism or their hopes of feudal paramountcy which led the Calverts on through Newfoundland and Maryland in the next generation.

The English separatists who were marked out for punishment in 1593 were given the choice of conforming or leaving the country after they had endured a certain period in jail. But many of those in Francis Johnson's London congregation refused to go abroad even if a Protestant nation would accept them. They would be cutting themselves off from a monarch to whom they felt, in spite of all, loyal. So in 1597 an attempt was made to provide them with a home in America. Captain Charles Leigh, a close sympathizer, proposed to take them to the Magdalen Islands in the St. Lawrence and there leave them to operate a fishery—mainly walrus, but cod as well. First visited in 1593 by George Drake, the islands were known by the English to attract both Basque and Breton fishing vessels. The would-be Pilgrim Fathers, for so we may call them, were to settle down, first, four of them on reconnaissance with a small ship's crew for the first winter, and next, the whole congregation, so as to start the collection of fish, oil, ivory, and skins early in the spring and scoop the pool from the other Europeans and the Indians who came from the mainland when good weather arrived. Francis Johnson and Daniel Studley sailed with Captain Leigh; George Johnson and John Clarke with Captain Van Harwick. Van Harwick missed the Magdalens and went aground on Cape Breton; he threatened to maroon his stiffnecked passengers when they would not approve of his taking to piracy. Meantime, the other ship had reached the Magdalens but was soon confronted by a combined force of Basques, Bretons, and Micmac Indians and driven from the islands. The sailors refused to take the ship to an alternative walrus fishery on Anticosti, so they returned, picked up the shipwrecked men at Cape Breton, and came home to the accompaniment of a hot exchange of theological arguments between the four disappointed pioneers. Gathering their congregation around them, they set up the Old Church at Amsterdam, as it came to be called after the Scrooby congregation came to Holland in 1607. From time

47

to time the project of going to America revived with them, and there is some evidence that it was they who inspired John Robinson, William Brewster, and William Bradford with the desire to move across the Atlantic which brought the Plymouth colony into being in 1620.

Once a group became seriously interested in establishing a colony, the simplest way to do it seemed to be to send a handful of soldiers, or more than that, to settle down inside a fortification. When a garrison was firmly established it could become the nucleus for whatever kind of colony the promoters might care to erect around it. This was the structure of both French colonies in Florida in the sixties, though neither worked well. Soldiers wanted to be fed, not to work to feed themselves; they had little interest in collecting trade goods when they did not get the profit of them directly. Consequently they got restless, dissolute, diseased, desperately anxious to get away from their unprofitable command.

In Ralph Lane's colony on Roanoke Island in 1585–1586 discipline was good and punitive action against the Indians decisive. Some plots of maize were even sown, but the men were too discontented to stay, and Lane could not hold them back when Drake offered them passage home in June, 1586. The military structure was also very much in evidence in Sagadahoc in 1608, though the commander was not as absolute as Lane apparently had been. But George Popham's men were discouraged by a long winter and lack of productive enterprise (except for one ship built). They too came home when they had an excuse. The Jamestown settlers were similarly in 1607 maintained as a military force: their lack of enterprise is mentioned by several writers. With some difficulty they were brought to fortify their settlement. They did plant a couple of ridges (hills) of corn, but they did not resist either boredom or disease. Repeatedly, from 1607 to 1616, it seemed that only chance prevented the soldierly colonists from slipping away, or the exercise of draconic punishment, bringing to them the bitter taste of army discipline. It can be argued that the military organization of the settlement worked against its early success; but it can also be urged that without the hard hand of the old captains and the severe law code of 1611 there would have been no colony at all.

One of the things the Spaniards always tried to find out about the early English colonial settlements on the American coast was whether they had any women amongst their numbers. If they had not, the Spaniards concluded that their purpose was piracy against the Spanish Indies, not, whatever King James might say, settlement in hitherto unclaimed land. The colony of men, their wives and their children, had a built-in formula for survival. Whether it would work depended on the framework, both physical and psychological.

The colony which John White brought out in 1587 was the first which had in it men, women, and children and which promised when reinforced to be a real basis for an enduring settlement. The reinforcements, a handful more of men and women who set out with White in 1588, were unable to complete the voyage and had to return to England. The settlers were consequently lost sight of and could not be found when White returned in 1590. It may be that their weakness, lack of effective government, the handicaps which the presence of women and children imposed on the men, and so on, may have led to the loss of many of the colonists, but it may also be that a substantial number endured alongside the Chesapeake Indians until, about 1606, Powhatan slaughtered Indians and whites, men and women alike. If the settlers did therefore survive in some organized form for the better part of twenty years, then their resilience, the sense of having homes and dependents to fight for and provide for, did indeed help the Lost Colonists to survive, and their disappearance at the hands of overwhelming and treacherous forces is no criticism of their effectiveness as a settlement. But this we cannot definitely say.

The first two women who came out on the third Virginia voyage in 1608 were no more than a nominal representation of their sex, but the appearance of women and children in some numbers in 1609 meant that the future of the Jamestown colony as a community, if it survived at all, might seem to be assured.

It can be argued that the Virginia settlement was not a viable one until there was land division as well as family settlement. This was not necessarily the case. The military character of the settlement in its early years did give it, in spite of the presence of some women and children, a transient aspect. It could be uprooted fairly easily because it had so few roots. Furthermore, the provision of food and necessities from the Company store was demoralizing to some of the settlers. At the same time, this provision of subsistence was not in any sense community of property: it was the treatment of civilians as well as soldiers, not as self-reliant individuals but as persons in a position of servitude, that made the difference in morale, not the existence of communal supplies as such.

The Virginia settlement had slowly to be fed with soldiers, farmers, farm laborers, craftsmen, administrators, landowners, institutions. Before 1620 Virginia was well on its way toward survival as a self-reliant community, but it had taken a long time, and, by the standards of the time, an almost incredibly high investment per settler to put it there. The Plymouth settlement of 1620 was the first English colony which had in it from the first most of the qualifications for survival. Here was a small community mutually bound together for a common purpose—even though all were not strict separating congregationalists. They had within them the capacity for self-regulation without the cruder forms of imposed coercion which had distinguished the attempts to bring order to the Jamestown settlement. Their organization had in it to begin with more community of goods and services than Jamestown, but here they were cooperatively applied. They had just enough capacity for force to provide protection without tempting them to kill too many Indians in the process. They had, in fact, the viability conveyed by collective responsibility. The traditional New England emphasis on the Pilgrims, now out of fashion, had thus a sound instinctual basis.

In what I have said so far it should be clear that there was no one formula for successful settlement. The English adventurers of the sixteenth century played variations on a considerable number of different approaches and solutions. That none of them produced a permanent settlement was as much accident as due to the faults of their planners and founders. Perhaps the only general point we can make is that most of the colonies attempted were too small, but even this was not inevitably a disqualification. Yet the seventeenth century did demonstrate a formula:

the more complete the social entity the better the chance of success; the more firm the ideological unity the greater the chance of early strength.

I have ranged hitherto rather widely over the background of settlement. It now remains to go back and to narrow the focus on the foundation of the Jamestown settlement itself. A great transformation occurred in the scale of English colonial activity with the issue of the Virginia Company charter on April 10, 1606. The ventures of Gosnold and Pring in 1602–1603 had been small-scale affairs for trading and exploration, with little or no coordination between them. If they revealed enough to point the way to settlement, and if Waymouth could be sent in 1605 to prepare the way for a new Catholic colony, yet there was no big money or large numbers of settlers involved. Bartholomew Gilbert's attempt in 1603 to discover the mouth of Chesapeake Bay was a failure, and if Newport looked in there on his way back from the West Indies in 1605 we do not know how much new information he could have picked up. Yet, while Waymouth in the autumn of 1605 had been scraping around for a small investment to start a settlement, some six months later there arose, full-blown, a dual Virginia Company (a northern one to exploit the Gosnold-Waymouth discoveries, a southern one for the Old Virginia of the Roanoke colonies, with a supervisory royal council to coordinate their activities and act as a watchdog for the state). We are still at a loss to know precisely how this came about. Recent work has done a good deal to elucidate the involvement of some of the 1607 settlers, such as Bartholomew Gosnold and John Smith, in the venture, but who were the architects of the great measure? Sir Thomas Smythe, the great London entrepreneur, certainly supplied the business confidence which led the City merchants to invest. Lord Chief Justice Popham and Lord Salisbury, the King's chief minister, between them were vitally important, and without them little would have been done. Yet we are not quite sure how it was tied together. Captain Waymouth himself may have been the one to get the King interested, and without his interest nothing could have happened. Sir Walter Cope, another official, may well have been the man who ran from sea captains to soldiers, from expert to expert (Edward Hayes to Richard Hakluyt), from merchant to statesmen (Smythe to Popham and Salisbury). But so much was done by word of mouth that we cannot tell precisely who was responsible for what. Certainly both Salisbury—as nominal High Steward of Plymouth and with his fiery friend Sir Ferdinando Gorges as commander of the Plymouth garrison—and Popham—with his grandson Thomas Hanham entrenched in the Plymouth plutocracy (such as it was) and his links with Bristol through having been Recorder—tied in the independent-minded western interests firmly with the Londoners.

There had to be several revisions of the Virginia Company charter before it worked at all efficiently—it never was a first-rate instrument for colonization. What it was excellent for was committing the English, at last, to a sustained program of settlement.

While the royal council did not operate very effectively in the day-to-day affairs of the Company, it was, I think, the one thing in the charter which gave reasonable assurance that state support for colonization would be maintained, even though it did not involve direct assistance from taxation. The element of national prestige which the maintenance of a colony, backed by such a body, conferred made it almost certain that the Crown would not abandon the Company in the face of Spanish threats. The very fact that the Spaniards managed to seize the "Richard," the first ship sent out by the westerners in 1606, and played a cat-and-mouse game with her men for several years, made Lord Salisbury and other members of the government determined not to give up the colonies. The long series of threats by Spain was set on one side with smooth talk rather than defiance, but the Spanish government proved unwilling to take the risk of war which the attempted destruction of the colony in 1607 or 1608 would probably have provoked.

By 1606 the various social and regional groupings which were interested in American colonization had been to some extent sorted out. The London merchants had become converted finally to speculative investment when it was seen that the new East India Company could make a profit; the western merchants were attracted into speculation by the sudden postwar boom in the Newfoundland fisheries. Dr. Theodore Rabb has drawn our attention to the scale of the landowners' investment in new speculative companies in the years after James's accession—no less than one-third of the landowning members of the Parliament of 1604–1611 being willing to invest in the open-ended mercantile venture which allowed money to work without requiring direct participation as a merchant. Besides, the landowners, and some merchants too, were interested in land speculation as such: certainly many were becoming interested in Irish land, and American land too might prove worthy of investment, with a possibility of resettlement there at a higher social and economic level than the investor enjoyed in England. We may, therefore, be justified in probing a little closer into economic and social motives, trying to bring out at least the major incentives as they presented themselves to the two major regional groupings represented in the Company.

What was the reason for the emphasis of the Londoners on a southern colony, why the stress by the western merchants on a northern? We have seen that there was an aristocratic desire for landed estates in North America; that demand was not linked very closely to one latitude rather than another, though perhaps it was directed a little more to areas where there were fewer rather than more Indian occupants who might interfere with the creation of new rural lordships. But it was the merchants' view of North America which was the decisive one. Without merchant capital, without the sustaining power of a strong economic program, a purely gentry colony might be very long in coming into existence. This, Gilbert's experiments had shown. The reason for the bias of the westerners, the merchants of Plymouth and Bristol, toward the American shore from Cape Cod northward was that their basic concern was with fish and oil and furs, and their colonizing interest was the expression of a need to find an area which could be exploited for these products all the year round, not merely in the short summer season. The objectives of the Londoners were different. In 1604 great hopes were pinned on the Levant and Spanish trades. The former would be free from Spanish interference in the Straits of Gibraltar; the latter would be open freely to English merchants for the first time since 1585. These hopes were soon, to some extent, qualified. North African pirates continued to take a fairly heavy toll from the Levant trade. In Spain and Portugal a maze of duties and lawsuits, and the hostility of officials, to some extent dimmed the hopes of high profits to be gained at San Lúcar, Seville, and Lisbon, and the outlook for Spanish commerce in the years immediately following the peace remained poor and uncertain. The English objective in the Iberian lands and the Mediterranean was to revive the trade in southern European products. The desire for a colony was therefore largely one for a base with an economy complementary to that of England so as to produce the sugar, wines, raisins, citrus fruit, rice, dyes (woad especially), possibly the leather and iron, which came mainly from the Iberian countries and their Atlantic island dependencies. Then, too, the peace excluded the English from the Spanish Indies. Perhaps the possession of a colony just outside the Spanish zone in North America would produce some of the minor riches of the Indies, like tobacco, dyes, and cotton, possibly even its major products, silver and gold, though opinion about potential mineral assets was inclined to be cautious. The foundation of the East India Company in 1600 and the return of its first fleet in 1603 had shown that London capital could produce all the spices, silks, and oriental dyes that England needed. A Caribbean base was ruled out for the time being by the treaty and by Spanish hostility and ruthlessness in dealing with intruders. A Virginian colony, in latitudes similar to that of the lapsed Roanoke settlement, was the best that could be hoped for. Both westerners and Londoners expected certain advantages from the timber resources of America—the westerners were concerned with pitch, tar, turpentine, masts, the chances of shipbuilding on the spot once a colony was established (the very first product of the Maine colony of 1607 was a ship); the

Londoners were concerned with clapboard for wainscot, staves for barrels (wine trade), cedar for fine cabinetmaking, the exploiting of the forests for smelting iron (either using local iron or else ore brought from England as ballast), and making glass and potash for soap—all activities which were becoming increasingly expensive at home as English timber was used up in increasing quantities. Sassafras to both was a medical panacea, but its significance was soon seen to be small.

Both westerners and Londoners had national aims too. The Spaniards were established in Florida: they might at any time move up the coast and occupy the sites which could serve English mercantile purposes. In the North the English had abandoned by 1602 any attempt to penetrate the St. Lawrence, since French activity there had increased at such a rate that it was clearly only a matter of time before permanent settlements were created. News that in 1604 the French had begun working down the Atlantic seaboard was clearly an incentive to get in first and preserve it from them.

These national aims also governed to some extent the character of the earliest settlements. With Spanish and French threats, however potential, to be met, it did not seem possible to send out purely civilian settlements as the first stage in the colonization. The nucleus of any settlement must be a body of militarily trained men under a degree of military discipline. Had the Indians been the sole reason for taking military precautions (and they were one), a modest program of arming and training civilians, and providing them with some military backbone, might have sufficed, as it did with the Pilgrims in 1620. But with professional European soldiers to be met with, potentially at least, men with professional training in the Low Countries and in the Irish wars were essential. They were available in considerable numbers now that peace had come. The problem which was not faced or solved in practice by the Virginia companies, and which brought them nearest to disaster, was how to exploit these military men productively. Beyond looking after a fort, once built, and making forays with exploring parties, it was hard to expect them (though it was expected of them) to turn laborers, craftsmen, merchants, and administrators. Some few did prove adaptable: the majority were too professionalized to remain anything but soldiers. Their uselessness (the word may be too emphatic, as they had some uses) was the main reason for the failure of the northern colony: it was the one, along with disease, which brought the southern colony several times to the verge of collapse.

There was this difference, too, between the westerners' and the Londoners' approach. The westerners hoped to develop colonies as a convenience. They did not greatly care about settlements as such and were quite willing to allow enterprising gentlemen or freedom-seeking Catholics, Separatists, or Puritans to do the pioneering for them, so long as merchant activities were left in their hands. When the Sagadahoc colony collapsed in 1608, they went on with their fishing and intermittent fur trading. With John Smith's help this New England commerce became quite profitable, though they still felt the need for shore bases to extend the season. As, in fact, the French did not move down the coast (Argall scotching in 1613 the attempt to start missions in Maine) they were not seriously impeded in carrying on profitable activities in American waters by the lack of American colonies, though their absence limited the scale on which they operated. The position of the Londoners was quite different. They could not achieve any of their aims without a colony. The whole basis of their economic program rested on agriculture, industry, and possibly mining, even though there was some subsidiary Indian trade to be obtained. If Jamestown was to be given up, the London merchant activities in America could pack up too. There was only one slight alternative open to them. They might give up settlement, though perhaps trying to keep a small port of call going, if they could revive full-scale trade under arms in the West Indies. Privateering had become just this by 1604: it had not ceased to be so at the peace, but it had to be a clandestine activity, in view of the desire of the Crown for peace and alliance with Spain, and was not capable of rapid expansion. Some London Company merchants would have been only too delighted to renew the open privateering war, but the device of the royal council for Virginia effectively prevented any such move. Unless and until royal policy cooled decisively against Spain, which it did not do until 1624, the Virginia Company of London was stuck with Jamestown (though they were able to launch out on a promising sideline in Bermuda in 1612) and had to make the best of it. These distinctions, then, were not unimportant in the survival of one Virginia settlement from 1607 onward. And they combined closely with the prestige factor already discussed.

When Christopher Newport reached England in July, 1607, after safely and rapidly establishing the first settlers in Jamestown, he reported not only that the country was extremely fertile but that it was apparently full of gold. This report caused tremendous excitement amongst the investors at first and an almost equally great outburst of disappointment when it was shown that the analysis of the supposed ore had once again been faulty. Sir Thomas Roe, nonetheless, spoke for the more cautious merchants and for the aristocratic investors as well when he said there was sufficient justification for "the honor and profit to our nation to make provincial to us a land ready to supply us with all necessary commodities naturally wanting to us, in which alone we suffer the Spanish reputation and power to swell over us." In other words, the economy of the new Virginia colony would complement that of Great Britain: in helping to make it do so King James might consider his new empire was well won. Newport went back to Jamestown; the hundred or so additional colonists he brought infused a new life into its dying frame. The crucial turning point had come and been passed. The road to Jamestown was not to be a mere track into a wilderness but a main road into colonial empire.

Shakespeare as an

Experimental Dramatist[*]

The Word Is "Boldly"

By MADELEINE DORAN

A FAVORITE theme for discussion in Shakespeare's day, and one that could be applied to various subjects, was Nature versus Art. Applied to poetry, the issue might be whether genius or art, native talent or the rules of the craft, were of more importance to the writer. No one denied the necessity of talent, of course, but there was room for great disagreement on the degree of knowledge of the art necessary or desirable to make best use of that talent. Few denied, either, that art should imitate nature (for this was the dominant aesthetic theory of the time), but there was room for dispute as to how the imitation should be done, whether within or without the frame of the laws

[*] Delivered on May 19, 1964. It had previously been given at the University of Kansas in the "Humanistic Lecture Series" on March 17 and at Vassar College on April 1. Miss Doran is a professor of English at the University of Wisconsin.

of poetry, supposedly found out by the ancients. From the fun Shakespeare makes of the rules and of various literary fads in *Love's Labor's Lost,* and from many hints in his other plays, most of us would place Shakespeare on the side of the "naturalists" against the "artsmen." Berowne forswears "taffeta phrases, silken terms precise, / Three-pil'd hyperboles, spruce affectation" in favor of "russet yeas and honest kersey noes." If the question were debated by the poets and dramatists who met at the Mermaid Tavern for good talk, one would imagine Shakespeare wittily defending nature and Ben Jonson contrarily holding forth on the urgency of art. But as in all such debates, the dichotomy is partly false. Any serious artist, however great his genius, must master the techniques of his craft—even if he has to forge new ones; else he is no artist and he will say nothing to his audience. Shakespeare knew well enough the importance of his art, as what he did with it shows. And he knew well enough, too, the trap into which such an argument is apt to fall. When Berowne argues learnedly against Navarre's proposal that the four young men devote three ascetic years to study, Ferdinand remarks shrewdly: "How well he's read, to reason against reading."

Nevertheless, the idea that Shakespeare was a rude, untutored genius, "warbling his native woodnotes wild," great in spite of his lack of art rather than because of his mastery of it, was a favorite idea about him in the late seventeenth and early eighteenth centuries. We are probably only now fully recovering from this idea in our estimate of him. The seeds of it were sown by Ben Jonson in his strictures against Shakespeare's easy composition, when he regretted that Shakespeare had never "blotted out line," and the idea grew in an age, the neoclassic or Augustan age, when the sense of form was strong and high value was placed on art that conformed (or seemed to conform) to rules. The impression Shakespeare gave to such an age of lack of art was partly owing to his bursting opulence in theme, mood, character, and language, an opulence appearing to a more disciplined age quite unrestrained by rule or taste; the impression was also partly owing to his carelessness, real or apparent, in many matters of detail. In our own time, our greater historical knowledge of the Elizabethan drama and of the Elizabethan stage, with their traditions and limitations, gives us perhaps a truer perspective with which to view Shakespeare's artistic achievement. We must agree that Shakespeare is not one of the great formalists among artists: he stands not with Racine or Molière, but with Euripides, say, or Aristophanes; with Chaucer and Cervantes rather than with Dante. But this is only to say that the form is unobtrusive, not that it does not exist. We must also agree that Shakespeare was not a theorist in the sense that his contemporary, Jonson, was. When Shakespeare says anything about art in general he echoes the aesthetic and critical commonplaces of his time, such as that poetry is a speaking picture, that it holds the mirror up to nature, and that it should teach as well as delight. These are principles which have very different meanings with different artists and in different practical contexts. Shakespeare's actual art, happily, was empirical, based on what was at hand—the Roman comedies studied in school, Italian comedies evidently sometimes performed, the diverse and still fluid and forming traditions of the English stage, and the tastes of the time in fiction and drama. This taste, strongly fostered by schoolboy education in rhetoric, was for lively and abundant action (unified or not), long moving speeches, witty dialogue, colorful pageantry—in short, for eloquence and "copy" (the Elizabethan word for copiousness, or fullness) in both words and things. In this practical shaping of his art, in which the guide lines, apart from plays in existence, came more from rhetoric than from theories about the drama, Shakespeare was like most contemporary English dramatists. But shaping there was—more with him than with most—and what that shaping was is the concern of this lecture.

The natural gifts which fitted Shakespeare to be a poet and a dramatist were a gift for storytelling, a gift for entering sympathetically into all kinds of human experience without losing his own moral direction, and a gift for language. He remembered, apparently, every word he ever heard or read, and he played with words zestfully to see what they could be made to do. He was like his time in this, only his gift was quintessential. He came along just at the right time to put these gifts to use in the most fruitful way—that is, just when the London professional theater had got established and was attracting a group of talented young writers—Lyly, Kyd, Greene, Nashe, Peele, and Marlowe. They were fashioning, out of a variety of traditions, both native and classical, the popular drama of the late years of Elizabeth's reign. Shakespeare learned a good deal from his immediate predecessors and contemporaries; most of the men I have named had begun to write only a year or two or three before he began. But he quickly established himself as a master in his own right, both by the range of his successful experiments in history, tragedy, and comedy and by his own unmistakable and individual style.

When I call Shakespeare an "experimental" dramatist, I

do not of course mean that he was a radical, either in making absolutely new beginnings or in rebelling against what had gone before. Not at all. We know well enough that he worked with tradition and convention (when there was any), not against it. But one sometimes hears the influences on him—Lyly's or Marlowe's or Greene's—talked about as if all he did was to fill up old bottles with a heady brew of fresh characters and poetry. This is not at all what he did. He had to make new bottles, even though he started by imitating the shapes that were in style. But the metaphor is misleading, since it makes form and content separate. Shakespeare worked, from beginning to end, to extend and shape his artistic medium of poetic drama so that it was adequate to his deepening insight into life. The work of art is, in fact, the insight. His work is almost always characterized by boldness, by willingness to take risks to achieve his ends. You will recall Menenius' reminder to Coriolanus when he goes out to meet the people and stand as "candidate" for the consulship. Menenius says, "Mildly, mildly," and Coriolanus, disgusted, but meaning to control himself, mutters, "The word is 'mildly.'" It is not Shakespeare's word; for him the word is "boldly."

I shall attempt to give you a general picture of Shakespeare's artistic accomplishment; but I shall stop to discuss two plays in some detail as illustrative examples—*Romeo and Juliet* and *King Lear,* an early tragedy and a late one.

Shakespeare's writing career, from 1588 or 1589 to 1613, a period of twenty-four or twenty-five years, in which he wrote thirty-seven plays, nearly coincides with the great age of the Elizabethan and Jacobean drama up to its crest. Such was the fertility of Shakespeare's mind that during these twenty-five years he rarely repeated himself. One can, of course, recognize recurrent formulas, especially in comedy, such as the two pairs of lovers and their comic triangles of shifting allegiance in *The Two Gentlemen of Verona, A Midsummer Night's Dream,* and *Twelfth Night.* But so distinctive in conception and execution, both in drama and in poetry, is each of these plays, that the similarity is less noticed than the difference. Shakespeare continued to experiment, not always successfully, but mainly so; always pushing out the boundaries of dramatic expression in history, tragedy, comedy, and in drama eluding the critics' imposed definitions. He tried to say things that could not be said within the formal boundaries of tragedy or comedy; therefore we have *Troilus and Cressida, Measure for Measure,* and *The Winter's Tale.* His verse constantly grew more varied, more subtle, and more daring. For all that, the whole artistic production is of a piece. The plays have, therefore, the marks of authentic great art: in each can be heard the style that is proper to Shakespeare alone, yet each play, in its difference from every other, has its own integrity.

We can illustrate the way in which Shakespeare was both traditional and original, the way in which he learned to exploit boldly his inherited medium, by looking at a play familiar to everyone, *Romeo and Juliet.* This play was written fairly early, that is, within the first six or seven years of his career; perhaps as early as 1591, but if so, revised into the form we know it no later than 1595. It is a useful play, therefore, to see how Shakespeare went about perfecting his art.

He took, first of all, a well-known story, one that had been told as an Italian prose *novella* or short story early in the sixteenth century, and that had been retold, with embellishments, in Italian, French, and English—and in prose narrative, in verse narrative, and on the stage. We even hear of an English play, but that was more than thirty years before Shakespeare's. To take a familiar story was according to the custom, even the precepts, of the time. Familiar stories, especially true tragic ones, were thought to have the advantage of credibility; and the Romeo and Juliet story was told by Da Porto and his followers as a true one. Moreover, training in composition in school was always training in imitation of what had already been written. Invention meant the finding and handling of material, not its first creation; originality lay in the alteration and embellishment of a theme, to give it new vitality and interest. (Shakespeare would never have been asked to write a theme on what he saw on his way to school; he would have been asked to write on what Hecuba said when she saw Pyrrhus, the son of Achilles, kill her husband, old King Priam of Troy, and he would have been expected to look first to see if Seneca or Vergil had said anything on the same subject.) For his tragedies and comedies, Shakespeare nearly always took a familiar story, from a romance, a novel, or a play—and he had an eye for good ones, such as those in *The Merchant of Venice, As You Like It, Hamlet, Othello,* or *King Lear.*

The story of *Romeo and Juliet* would seem to be foolproof to begin with: the story of two very young people who are deeply in love but who have the world of circumstance all against them from the start. Characteristically, Shakespeare's changes go with the grain of the original story; they do not alter its direction but rather deepen its essential irony. In the earlier versions, the progress of the story—the falling in love, the courtship, the secret marriage, the drawing of Romeo into the feud with his accidental killing of a Capulet, the banishment from Verona, Old Capulet's plan to marry Juliet to Count Paris, Juliet's desperate appeal to Friar Laurence and the friar's stratagem of the sleeping potion, Juliet's burial and the final accidents in timing which result in the suicide of the lovers —all this, I say, occupied nine months. Shakespeare reduced the time (which he very precisely marked from day to day, and sometimes from hour to hour) to four and a half days—that is, from Sunday afternoon to the dawn of Friday morning. Now this shortening of the times makes the action of the play far less realistic and far less credible than the action in the original story. What Shakespeare did was to sacrifice ordinary realism to speed, for the purpose of gaining emotional intensity and a heightened dramatic irony. This was a bold adaptation of narrative, with its more relaxed pace, to drama. No preceding popular dramatist had done anything like this in transferring narrative to the stage, and very few in the period ever *were* to do it. The general practice was to let a borrowed story take its course, without too much concern about time, place, or motivation. But Shakespeare was to continue to experiment boldly with time; *Othello* is a later example of great compression. In *Romeo and Juliet,* Shakespeare not only speeded up the action but folded it back on itself: he introduced Tybalt and Paris near the beginning, so as to give the audience an expectant awareness of trouble to come; he placed the duel and the killing of Tybalt on the afternoon between Romeo's wedding to Juliet and the wedding night, so that this first intimate meeting is poignant with the knowledge of separation. The coming tragedy casts its shadow before it. This creation of expectancy, and the sharing of secrets with the audience so that we may savor the full irony in any situation, whether it be tragic or comic, is one of the primary techniques of Shakespeare's art.

Another thing to notice in *Romeo and Juliet* is what Shakespeare did to the characters. In the Italian *novelle,* character, or personality, as we think of it after a long experience with psychological novels, is not very important, and generally was not in the flood of stories inherited from the Middle Ages; in the *Romeo and Juliet* story character was merely typical—a pair of young lovers, intense and thoughtless, and undifferentiated from any other pair; an irascible and somewhat tyrannical father cut to a conventional pattern of old age; a nurse or duenna readily drawn, as all duennas are, into intrigue for her young mistress; several headstrong young men touchy about their honor; and a friar who was merely a piece of machinery to move the plot. The characters filled their required rôles in the story and that was enough. Not because he was expected to do so, but because he had a gift for doing it, Shakespeare gave depth and individuality to the principal characters, touched even Friar Laurence with a breath of life, and invented an altogether new character in Mercutio (who had been no more than a man with cold hands, named "Marcuccio Guercio," in the source). But Shakespeare's Mercutio is not just a new character to swell the scene; he is brought in to complicate the plot, to intensify by his interference and by his being killed the overwhelming sense of irony in the misfortune that besets Romeo. Moreover, while Mercutio is on the scene he introduces a different point of view toward love, for he is a witty scoffer. Mercutio enriches the play, then, in three ways, all characteristic of Shakespeare—in himself as a vivid character; in complicating the action for ironic effect; and in introducing a different and even contrary point of view, one which does not destroy the dominant note, the tragedy of star-crossed love, but which places it in a wider context of diverse human experience and increases its poignancy by contrast. This ability to entertain a variety of points of view toward human experience without losing either moral or artistic direction is, I am tempted to say, almost peculiar to Shakespeare among the dramatists of his time; at least it is his gift pre-eminently.

Another thing that Shakespeare has done, in plotting *Romeo and Juliet* for the stage, is to make scenes which act as strong structural markers. One set is the three scenes of the feud—in the public square at the very beginning, in the same place at the climax of the duel in the middle, and at the tomb at the end of the play. Another set is the scenes between the lovers—especially the wooing by moonlight with Juliet at the window and the separation at dawn, again at Juliet's window. These repetitions with variations give us a sense of pattern and satisfy us in the same way as does the return of a theme in music.

There is also, here, an exploitation of setting—the Capulet garden, the public square, the tomb—to emphasize theme and mood. Much of Shakespeare's setting had to be created in the poetry itself, for his stage was lighted by the daylight sky and was relatively bare, at least of painted scenery. Yet he was fond of night scenes. Notice how Romeo and Juliet keep us aware by small touches that it is night and that Romeo is dangerously inside the Capulet orchard. Juliet says,

> How cam'st thou hither . . . ?
> The orchard walls are high and hard to climb,
> And the place death, considering who thou art,
> If any of my kinsmen find thee here.

Again, Juliet:

> Thou knowest the mask of night is on my face;
> Else would a maiden blush bepaint my cheek
> For that which thou hast heard me speak tonight.

And Romeo swears his love:

> Lady, by yonder blessed moon I swear,
> That tips with silver all these fruit-tree tops.

Contrast the hot summer afternoon on which the feud breaks out. Benvolio says,

> I pray thee, good Mercutio, let's retire.
> The day is hot, the Capulets abroad,
> And if we meet, we shall not scape a brawl,
> For now, these hot days, is the mad blood stirring.

Not only direct description or allusive reference but the imagery itself emphasizes the contrast between light and dark which is used thematically throughout the play. When Romeo, in the Capulet garden, sees Juliet open her window, he says:

> But soft! What light through yonder window breaks?
> It is the East, and Juliet is the sun!

Compare his lines at the end, when he breaks open the door of the Capulet tomb, to find Juliet lying within:

> A grave? O, no, a lanthorn, slaught'red youth,
> For here lies Juliet, and her beauty makes
> This vault a feasting presence full of light.

In this way setting and imagery together mark the central tragic irony of the play: "O, now be gone!" Juliet says as the dawn brings the end of their wedding night: "More light and light it grows." To which Romeo replies: "More light and light—more dark and dark our woes!"

The poetry in *Romeo and Juliet* is used also, properly, for the lyric expression of love and despair. But the emotions are not just "expressed"; passion is contained and given beauty by the formality and ornamental richness of the verse, as in the meeting sonnet which the two divide between them. It begins:

> If I profane with my unworthiest hand
> This holy shrine, the gentle fine is this:
> My lips, two blushing pilgrims, ready stand
> To smooth that rough touch with a tender kiss.

And you all know how, after the interchange between the young people of the parts of the sonnet, the couplet ends with a kiss.

> *Jul.*   Saints do not move, though grant for prayers' sake.
> *Rom.*   Then move not while my prayer's effect I take.

In the English film of the play (the one filmed in Italy) the titillation which was produced by the overlong teasing play of eyes between the lovers, and then by the avoidance —of all things—of the kiss at the end of this sonnet of meeting, was quite false to Shakespeare's sense of the scene, which is both shy and hesitantly bold, adoring and witty. Having kissed her lips, Romeo says,

> Thus from my lips, by thine my sin is purg'd.
> *Jul.*   Then have my lips the sin that they have took.
> *Rom.* Sin from my lips? O trespass sweetly urg'd!
> Give me my sin again!

This is an excuse, of course, to kiss her a second time. Juliet ends the interchange with the disarming "You kiss by the book."

The formality appears again in the *aubade* or dawn song on the morning of their separation. This scene of parting is not, any more than the scene of meeting, designed to exploit sensuality, as is often done in representation on the stage or in films, by setting the scene within the bedroom. Shakespeare sets it at the window viewed from outside. It is a scene of moving irony. The longing and the pain together are exquisitely restrained in the counterpoint of lark and nightingale played between the lovers.

Jul.   Wilt thou be gone? It is not yet near day.
      It was the nightingale, and not the lark,
      That pierc'd the fearful hollow of thine ear.
      Nightly she sings on yond pomegranate tree.
      Believe me, love, it was the nightingale.
Rom. It was the lark, the herald of the morn;
      No nightingale. Look, love, what envious streaks
      Do lace the severing clouds in yonder East.
      Night's candles are burnt out, and jocund day
      Stands tiptoe on the misty mountain tops.
      I must be gone and live, or stay and die.

There is formality again in Juliet's several arias and in Romeo's last great apostrophe to Juliet and to death. At the same time, Shakespeare was exploring, in Mercutio's lively and expressive prose, a relatively new medium—for prose with the accent of everyday speech was not common in the theater except for low, very low, comedy. Shakespeare's prose was to achieve greatness in the Falstaff scenes in the Henry IV plays later in the decade.

Romeo and Juliet is not perfect. There are places where invention labors and where the verse is frigid; compared with the later, greater tragedies, its tragic theme is a limited one. But for all that, the play is truly remarkable in the way in which fable, character, setting, and poetry all work together toward a common end—the end which *is* the work of art, the tragedy of the star-crossed lovers. Another way of putting this, in more Elizabethan terms, is to say that the play excels in invention, disposition, and eloquence, and that it embodies the artistic ideal of unity in variety.

Shakespeare was to go on to greater tragedies later— tragedies offering a wider range than *Romeo and Juliet* of vital characters; profounder insights into human passion, into the moral dilemmas men face, into the ironies in their destiny; and richer and more varied expression in verse and in prose. But *Romeo and Juliet* does point the way to Shakespeare's characteristic methods of working: first, his choice of a strong and usually well-known story, sometimes from supposedly true tales of private life (as with *Othello*), more often from history (as with *Macbeth* and the Roman plays), or from historical legend (as with *Hamlet* and *King Lear*); secondly, his bold shaping of the story to fit the stage and to deepen its tragic meaning; thirdly, his creation of striking effects at the expense of realism (notably in *Othello* and *Lear*); fourthly, his creation of characters who speak with the accent of life and so engage us in their sufferings and problems, even in their evil (as with Iago and Edmund); fifthly, his enriching of the action with different and even contrary points of view toward the central issues of life; sixthly, his management of setting and time to reinforce action, theme, and mood; finally, and above all, his exploitation of the resources of the language—diction, imagery, syntax, prosody—the chief tool by which he does all these other things.

At about the same time as he was writing *Romeo and Juliet,* that is, about 1594 or 1595, when he was thirty or thirty-one, he also found his way in comedy. This was in *A Midsummer Night's Dream,* in which, as in *Romeo and Juliet,* action, character, setting, and poetry all cooperate in a satisfying whole, and this time the whole is made from rather more diverse materials—a Theseus from Greek and Roman and medieval legend, lovers from Renaissance fiction and drama, fairies from romance and folklore and contemporary literature, craftsmen from Stratford—and perhaps from the rhetoric books. These things are blended into a mixture of high comedy and low, romance and farce, fun and fantasy, dream and reality, poetry and prose. Shakespeare had tried Roman comedy in *The Comedy of Errors,* Italian comedy in *The Taming of the Shrew,* and Lylyan comedy in *Love's Labor's Lost* and had found them too hard of surface for his sympathies and his poetry. The tradition he was to exploit in comedy was the popular tradition of romance—the kind of story that takes well-meaning people through trial and tribulation to a happy ending. The romance in *A Midsummer Night's Dream,* a comedy of Blind Cupid, is somewhat qualified. But Shakespeare made in that play an important discovery—the discovery, that is, of the usefulness of a scene removed from the world of reality. Here it is a moonlit wood inhabited by fairies, those amoral minor powers that bear so much sway in human domestic affairs. Later the place was to be the Forest of Arden, or a sheepcote in Bohemia, or an enchanted island in the Mediterranean. In every instance it is a place where the characters may think and act outside the normal restraints and proprieties of everyday society. Shakespeare makes them, and us, see things in a different perspective—not to let them escape, but to send them back to their homes in city and court a good deal the wiser. In this early comedy the topsy-turvy experiences of the night, when every lover was at cross-purposes, seem to the awakened lovers like a Midsummer Night's dream. But they know now what trothplight and fidelity are and return to the responsible world of Theseus to enter marriage and a new life. This play thus prefigures the comic vision of Shakespeare's comedies to come.

Still another line of experiment in these early years was with history—far more intractable than fiction, because it contains few ready-made plots and is far too cluttered up with people, events, and irrelevancies to turn readily into drama. Shakespeare sought in various ways to bring it on the stage with a shape and a meaning—in chronicle, as in the Henry VI plays, with a sense of cyclic rise and fall of princes; in melodramatic tragedy, as in *Richard III*—a tragedy touched with Senecan nemesis, fury, ghosts, and rhetoric; in psychological tragedy, as in *Richard II;* in dramatic epic as in *Henry V;* or as a great interplay and clash of personalities in a political setting as in the Henry IV plays. I have already noted, in connection with *Romeo and Juliet,* Shakespeare's sense of what might be called the genius of a story. In history this awareness is expressed in a sense of the meaning of event for the people taking part in it. Hence the variety of treatment in the history plays. At the same time the whole sequence of plays covering the struggle for power beginning with the deposition of Richard II and ending with the death of Richard III at the hands of the first Tudor king made a kind of epic of English history in the fifteenth century, an epic unified by Shakespeare's strong patriotism and his conservative political doctrine that social order depended on a strong and responsible monarchy. Such a plan was certainly not conceived from the beginning but was loosely achieved in the process of composition.

As a reminder, before turning to the great tragedies, and especially *King Lear,* I should like to come back for a moment to our initial theme of nature and art. Shakespeare had par excellence the native gifts his age admired—the teeming imagination, the fecund invention, the keen-edged wit. His art, therefore, was always copious and various, always exuberant. But unlike some of his contemporaries with gifts similar in kind if less in intensity and in abundance (say Thomas Nashe, or Christopher Marlowe), he had an architectonic sense—that is a gift for co-ordination and emphasis. And he learned by practice not so much to tame his invention, to subdue it to the limits of the theater (though some taming was necessary), as to use it boldly, to extend the range of the very possibilities of drama. He was not always a careful artist, never a cautious one. He gets away with things he has no right to, like the hunchback Gloucester's wooing of Anne in *Richard III,* or like another Gloucester's falling flat on the stage (in *Lear*) in the sight of the audience and yet being made to believe, through Edgar's persuasive eloquence, that he has fallen off Dover Cliff. Shakespeare enjoys setting himself hurdles to clear. He likes to begin a play with the hero shown unsympathetically and at a marked disadvantage, as in *Richard II* or *Othello* or *Antony and Cleopatra,* and then to bring the audience round to sympathy or even admiration. He wins us, all the world to nothing! In art nothing succeeds like success, and in Shakespeare the daring attempt usually pays off. When it does, the gain to the audience in delight or excitement is enormous.

His art grew with his vision of human experience, and

so, conservative and traditional as in some senses he was, he never stopped experimenting. His tragedies alone show this; every one of the great seven, from *Julius Caesar* in 1599 (when he was thirty-five) through *Coriolanus* in 1608 or 1609 (when he was about forty-five), is different in theme and form and technique. For example, *Julius Caesar* is a tragedy set in the real world of politics, its motives and its issues as mixed, as impossible to reduce to a simple formula of right and wrong, as these things are in the world we live in. In its realism of setting and character *Hamlet* is not unlike *Julius Caesar,* but the issues are primarily ethical, evil is recognizable and nameable, and the inward intensities of decision are increased. *King Lear,* unlike either, is a vast drama of good and evil, its scene and its figures larger than life and full of symbolic suggestion. Nor is the style at all the same. In place of the swift, supple verse, and equally supple prose, of *Hamlet,* comes the slower paced, sometimes craggy verse of *Lear,* with its imperatives, its inversions, its archaic diction. Action and poetry strain the resources of stage and performer. And then, in another contrast, comes the huge canvas of *Antony and Cleopatra,* its splendors and its intimacies conveyed in a poetry for the ear composed in sheer delight.

If we wish to choose the tragedy from this great period which shows Shakespeare at his most daring, and at probably his greatest reach of vision and of art, we shall take *King Lear.* A very brief summary of the plot will make the comments easier to follow. As you know, *Lear* is the story of an old king, an essentially good man but autocratic in his pride and ignorant of himself and others, who decides to divide his kingdom among his three daughters and to give the choicest portion to the one who loves him best—

sure beforehand that this will be the youngest, best-loved daughter, Cordelia. The two wicked elder daughters, Goneril and Regan, flatter him hypocritically and gain the whole kingdom between them; for the loyal youngest daughter, who speaks simply and honestly, is cast off. He learns the truth in a cruel experience at the hands of the elder daughters that costs him his reason; he is restored to sanity and finds the ultimate truth of love in the perfect and selfless love of Cordelia. His story is paralleled by that of the lesser figure of Gloucester and his two sons—the utterly evil Edmund the Bastard, who becomes the master-villain of the plot, and the faithful and loving Edgar, who heals his father as Cordelia does Lear, and who becomes the champion of Lear against Edmund and the evil daughters in the final action. But though the evil forces are destroyed, Gloucester dies of heartbreak at the discovery of the constant love of the son he has wronged, and, Lear, who has a moment of joy with Cordelia before she is killed by a prison guard, dies of this new and dreadful shock.

I have outlined the play thus barely, with much omitted, to bring out certain things about it. The core of it is an old and simple folk tale, the loving-like-salt story fused with the Cinderella theme of the youngest-best. The father poses a question to his three daughters: "Which of you loves me best?" The first answers, "I love you more than life." The second, "I love you more than all the world." The third, and youngest, "I love you as much as salt." The father must learn the value of salt by going without it before he realizes that this youngest daughter is the one who loves him truly. In the chronicle histories, in which the Lear story had been grafted onto early British legendary history, the youngest daughter was made to say, "I love you as much as you are worth." Shakespeare's Cordelia says, "I love you according to my bond." The answer is in every case a riddle, put with some irony; both the riddle and the irony the father fails to understand. In Shakespeare's play, Lear has to learn what loving according to Cordelia's "bond" means—the bond of love between father and daughter; he has to learn it by being deprived of it and by being subjected to the hate of the other daughters. In the process, he learns the whole meaning of "bonds" in society. The fairy-tale characteristics of the fundamental story Shakespeare does not suppress but exploits—in the drawing of the characters in such a way as to emphasize their determined rôles in the story, in the neglect of preparatory motivation, in the absolutes of phrasing and of choice: "Know that we have divided in three our kingdom"; "Tell me, my daughters, / Which of you shall we say doth love us most?" "Nothing can come of nothing. Speak again."

Realism of representation Shakespeare rejects for fairy tale, but fairy tale stretched and involuted and ramified so as to reach into all the attitudes and values inherent in human relationships; fairy tale converted, moreover, into tragedy. Fairy tales usually have a happy ending, and the Lear story did, in the several places Shakespeare found it told. In this one respect, in an exception that "proves" (or tests) the rule, Shakespeare turned against the current of his source story. He knew what he was doing and did it with characteristic daring. He was helped in the conversion by a tragic story he found in Sidney's *Arcadia*—the story of the "old kind king of Paphlagonia and his unkind son," which he interwove with the Lear story. This descriptive phrase states the primary theme of the play: *unkindness*—unkindness, through vanity and ignorance, of

two essentially kind fathers to their true and loyal children; unkindness, through deliberate malice and the quest
for selfish power, of the false children to their parents. But
"unkindness" means, in Elizabethan English, "unnatural-
ness." To behave according to Nature, that is to behave
according to one's "kind," is, for man, who is a moral
being endowed with reason and possessing an immortal
soul, to behave with kindness, decency, regard for others—
in short, with humanity. For a man to be unkind is to
behave like a beast without reason or moral knowledge; to
act on purely selfish impulse or for selfish ends is to break
the natural bonds that form society and make civilized life
possible. In the myth of Prometheus, as Plato tells it in the
Protagoras, Prometheus' gift of fire and the teaching of the
arts to mankind were not enough; Zeus had to add justice
and reverence in order for men to live together in social
harmony. The theme of unkindness in the stories of the
two families Shakespeare has widened to encompass not
only Lear's kingdom but the world. He suggests a society
in which all bonds are broken—in domestic life, in political life, and in religion—a society, therefore, which seems
to be returning, through cruelty and lust and unrestrained
selfishness, to savagery and chaos:

Love cools, friendship falls off, brothers divide. In cities,
mutinies; in countries, discord; in palaces, treason; and the
bond crack'd 'twixt son and father. . . . We have seen the
best of our time. Machinations, hollowness, treachery, and all
ruinous disorders follow us disquietly to our graves.

Shakespeare's problem, in handling this vast theme, was
to universalize the story without losing the immediacy of
particular experience at the center. This, I suppose, is the
problem of all poetry. But this end may be achieved in

very different ways. In his day, Shakespeare might still, perhaps, have chosen allegory, as Spenser did, that is, the working out of a theme in a fable in which the characters personify abstract ideas. The morality play technique was not wholly dead, and it might have been revived in a significant way. But Shakespeare always worked the other way round—from the living person in a living experience outward to the ethical implication of the experience. He usually chose the method of *Hamlet* or *Othello,* in which the experience of lifelike characters in a realistic setting is so vividly and sympathetically presented that it comes home to us: and this coming home, or recognition, constitutes its universal validity. But in *Lear,* trying perhaps to reach further, Shakespeare does a somewhat different thing. He follows the hint of fairy tale to simplify the characters. He starts from the center as usual: Goneril is not Lady Cruelty, Cruelty personified—she is a cruel woman, but also an imperious, conniving, and lustful one. Kent is not Sir Loyalty, but a man whose loyalty is the essential trait of a fine and honest character. All the characters are recognizable people, who speak with the accent of life—a fact which makes them all the more telling; but they are simplified and concentrated, and they separate, some standing on the side of good, some on the side of evil. This concentration and alignment makes for emphasis on theme. Nevertheless, at the center of the play is the thoroughly human experience of Lear, who is of mingled stuff, like all of us. He is proud, vain, passionate, but also generous and well-meaning; the enlargement of the scale of his passions universalizes the issue without losing the fundamental realism of the experience.

The doubling of the experience is another way to universalize it. To repeat, with variations, Lear's experience in Gloucester's, is to suggest that it is a general experience in families. But the Gloucester story is not simply repetition; it is best expressed in a musical metaphor—the repetition of a theme in another key, sometimes a minor key. (Musical metaphors have a way of coming to mind with reference to *King Lear*.) Lear's experience—the pride which refuses to admit his mistake, his gnawing remorse, his unwilling recognition of his daughters' betrayal, the suffering that brings awareness of the suffering of others—is treated with complexity and in detail. Action in the Gloucester plot, on the other hand, is done swiftly, almost crudely, without much attempt at credibility. And Lear's inner struggle and loss of reason are matched with the sudden violent disillusion of Gloucester in the savage blinding on the stage. No doubt this is partly a matter of keeping the primary emphasis on the main story, where it belongs; but this handling serves like strong bold strokes to reinforce, as in painting or drawing, certain colors or structural lines. The woodcuts of Dürer or the etchings of Rembrandt often furnish illustrations of this technique in graphic art. I have spoken thus much of structure, because the complexity of *Lear* sometimes keeps critics from noticing the strong timbers in the building—less exposed than in *Romeo and Juliet* or *Othello*, but nevertheless there.

I shall merely remind you quickly of other ways in which Shakespeare has suggested universal meanings. He has constantly repeated key words, like "Nature," "natural," "kindness," "gratitude," "loyal," and their opposites. He has used iterative imagery (as we have been much told of late) with especial fullness and effect—particularly the imagery of savage animals: "tigers, not daughters"; "how sharper than a serpent's tooth it is to have a thankless child"; "Ingratitude! . . . More hideous when thou show'st thee in a child / Than the sea-monster"—an imagery to suggest a human ferocity worse than that of beasts of prey, which are only following their kind. Another iterative pattern is the imagery of physical torture, which gives poetic intensity to the physical and mental suffering exhibited in the action: "I am bound / Upon a wheel of fire, that mine own tears / Do scald like molten lead"; "He hates him / That would upon the rack of this tough world / Stretch him out longer." Above all, Shakespeare has made the storm an extension of the experience of the characters. The poetry in which it is created affects us as an orchestration of the turmoil in Lear's mind and of the chaos in society. The play is one of violent contrasts, violent tensions, violent wrenchings, within the human mind and without it.

The imagery and the storm are poetic means of giving universal meaning; they speak to us subliminally and affectively. But Shakespeare has also given a large part in the play, probably larger than in any other, even *Hamlet,* to what Aristotle would call *dianoia,* or thought, in the form of general reflections on the obligations of power, the relation of power to justice, the relation of the gods to man, the needs of naked man and of civilized man. Having no formal chorus, Shakespeare has created choric characters, like the Fool, and like Edgar when he is in disguise as mad Tom, who direct our sympathies and guide our judgments in illumining the moral choice, the questions of value, the implications about man and society, which the characters in action keep continually before us. Both the Fool and Edgar do more than this, of course. One thing they do is to touch us deeply from time to time with a haunting lyric note: "Out went the candle, and we were left darkling"; "Still through the hawthorn blows the cold wind"; "Child Rowland to the dark tower came."

All this, apart from the general reflections, may be called the method of symbolism. The term is valid provided one does not turn it, on the one hand, into a radical philosophic symbolism, which reads life itself as merely a set of symbols for the true reality outside it; or, on the other hand, into the loose symbolism of modern symbolic poetry, which will be sharp in its emotional suggestion, but which is vague in ideational content, and which therefore allows considerable freedom of interpretation to the individual reader. The symbols in *King Lear*—primarily the setting and the imagery, but also, to a certain extent, the enlarged and simplified characters and some of the actions—limit and reinforce one another. They start from the tragic fable and return to enrich it.

The verse itself moves with the quality of the experience. As an example, take Lear's style. The play opens with the imperatives of his position and his pride:

> Meantime we shall express our darker purpose.
> Give me the map there. Know that we have divided
> In three our kingdom.

Or,

> Peace, Kent!
> Come not between the dragon and his wrath.

These imperatives are heard again in his dreadful curses:

> Hear, Nature, hear! dear goddess, hear!
> Suspend thy purpose, if thou didst intend
> To make this creature fruitful.

Into her womb convey sterility;
Dry up in her the organs of increase;

and so on. They are heard in his defiance of the warring
elements:

Blow, winds, and crack your cheeks! rage! blow!
You cataracts and hurricanoes, spout
Till you have drench'd our steeples, drown'd the cocks!
You sulph'rous and thought-executing fires,
Vaunt-couriers to oak-cleaving thunderbolts,
Singe my white head! And thou, all-shaking thunder,
Strike flat the thick rotundity o' th' world,
Crack Nature's moulds, all germains spill at once,
That make ingrateful man!

and still again in the irrational fancies of his mania:
"Arraign her first, 'tis Goneril!" and "Let them anatomize
Regan" and "Read thou this challenge; mark but the
penning of it." But when Lear is healed, the imperatives
fall away in a simplicity of statement that is the height of
art. When, with rest and music and the ministrations of
Cordelia, Lear has come back to sanity, he asks her,

Be your tears wet? Yes, faith. I pray weep not.
If you have poison for me, I will drink it.
I know you do not love me; for your sisters
Have, as I do remember, done me wrong.
You have some cause, they have not.

All of Cordelia's immeasurable love is in her reply: "No
cause, no cause." When she asks him, "Will't please your
Highness walk?" Lear answers,

You must bear with me.
Pray you now, forget and forgive. I am old and foolish.

In *King Lear,* written probably at forty-one, as in
Romeo and Juliet, written at about thirty-one, character,

setting, imagery, diction, and verse co-operate with the story to engage us wholly—which is a way of saying "to give the story meaning"—only now in ways immeasurably deeper and richer. What I have been saying is that Shakespeare had a strong sense of both the ethos and the pathos of a story; and that at the same time he had the courage to exploit his sense of the story at whatever cost to superficial realism or consistency. To put it in another way, I have been saying that his imaginative penetration into experience was matched with a bold inventiveness in all the resources of his art.

What Shakespeare did in *King Lear* was not like anything that had ever been done on the English stage, or that ever was to be done. One might suppose that he would have rested there. But it was only his Seventh Symphony. Three great tragedies followed—*Macbeth, Antony and Cleopatra,* and *Coriolanus*—each quite different in conception and tone. In the late romances, *Pericles, Cymbeline, The Winter's Tale,* and *The Tempest,* he took up again the romantic material of the earlier comedies, careless now of its improbabilities, and stretched it into new shapes and new meanings. His boldness, amounting to greater indifference to rule, increased with age and experience. (Not that the age was a great one—we sometimes forget that he was writing these romances between his forty-fifth and his forty-eighth year.) In his verse he discovered new dissonances and new harmonies. In compressed and knotted syntax, he sometimes sacrificed lucidity to concentration and complexity of meaning and euphony to harshness or muscularity. Hear Antony's limited apology for his wife Fulvia's wars against Octavius Caesar:

> So much uncurbable, her garboils, Caesar,
> Made out of her impatience—which not wanted
> Shrewdness of policy too—I grieving grant
> Did you too much disquiet.

Yet sometimes he opened out his verse into pellucid simplicity and haunting cadence. Thus Ferdinand, on the beauty of the wedding masque arranged by Ariel:

> This is a most majestic vision, and
> Harmonious charmingly.

And art is in some sense discovery—discovery for the artist and discovery for his viewers or hearers or readers. The greatness of Shakespeare in this sense is that for him there was no stopping point. His art grew with his awareness. In one of his latest plays, *The Tempest*— a play which shows what man at his best may do with his power of moral choice—one of the characters, faithful old Gonzalo, sums up the play:

> In one voyage
> Did Claribel her husband find at Tunis,
> And Ferdinand her brother found a wife
> Where he himself was lost; Prospero his dukedom
> In a poor isle; and all of us ourselves
> When no man was his own.

Shakespeare's whole artistic career, from first to last, was a voyage of discovery—for him, and for us.

Shakespeare and the

Tudor Perception of History*

By ARTHUR R. HUMPHREYS

AS Coleridge wrote in the *Biographia Literaria,*

No man was ever yet a great poet without being at the same time a profound philosopher. For poetry is the bloom and fragrancy of all human knowledge, human thoughts, human passions, emotions, language.

In no sphere is this more true of Shakespeare than in that of his history plays. Though not formally an historian, or formally a scholar, Shakespeare shows great intellectual grasp in the field of history, and great understanding of, and feeling for, the condition of human life in historical actions. His poetry in the history plays is indeed the bloom and fragrancy of human knowledge, thoughts, and passions about great actions of the past; he has a deep instinctive though hardly formulated philosophy about them, and be-

* Delivered on September 13, 1964. Mr. Humphreys is a professor of English at the University of Leicester.

yond any other Elizabethan writer he seems to express the deeper instincts of his time and to form for later generations their conception of past ages—Coleridge said that no man would object if his son learnt his history from Shakespeare. Particular episodes may live as vividly in the pages of others, as the last fight of the "Revenge" does in Raleigh's *Fight about the Iles of the Açores,* but the only non-Shakespearean work that has affected the national consciousness on anything like the scale of Shakespeare's is, I suppose, Foxe's *Acts and Monuments,* or *Book of Martyrs.* And even that, powerful though its sway for three centuries, has lost its general efficacy in the fourth: its quatercentenary last year occasioned no popular celebrations, as far as I know, though it evoked some scholarly tributes—and if any tribute to Shakespeare in 1964 proves a better offering to its subject than Professor William Haller's *Foxe's Book of Martyrs and the Elect Nation* was in 1963, Shakespeare, turning in his grave with some of this year's goings-on, will let his perturbed spirit rest with pleasure.

Shakespeare's histories are the culmination of a great trend of Tudor interest, the crowning achievement of the age's desire to realize the past as a living body of tradition, experience, and precept. They are a crowning achievement in two senses: they climax that desire qualitatively, by throwing into the shade every other Elizabethan history play, Marlowe's *Edward II* included; and they are a crowning achievement chronologically—few history plays were written after 1600, as though the great impulse had now expended itself. From a critical point of view, the fact that these plays so reflect the need of their age may be irrelevant; were they not good plays for dramatic reasons these extraneous considerations would not make them so, any more than the fact that the tenth canto of the second book of Spenser's *Faerie Queene* embodies the cherished legends of British antiquity makes it good poetry. To expound "The Spirit of the Age" is a different thing from practicing criticism. Yet the presence of such a spirit will be a support to a great artist, especially one who provides for popular taste. Shakespeare's histories embody a peculiar wealth of national story and character: here, more than anywhere else, he stands for his countrymen, then and now, and his achievement would have been less had it not been the climax of a great tradition.

About this tradition many things can be and have been said. I want at the moment to stress only its antiquity and its volume. Professor Lily B. Campbell's book, *Shakespeare's "Histories": Mirrors of Elizabethan Policy* (1947), is a rich and absorbing study of the whole Renaissance field of historiography, to which I gladly acknowledge my debts; Dr. Louis B. Wright has included in his *Middle-Class Culture in Elizabethan England* (1936) a lively and detailed account of how the ordinary Elizabethan reader came by his historical reading through the multiplied publication of chronicles, translations, ballads, and woodcuts; and Professor Haller, in the study of Foxe to which I have referred, has given a fascinating account of the great historians of the Tudor and Caroline ages. Tudor history is an accumulation of many ages of tradition, going back through the sixteenth-century chroniclers like Holinshed, Stow, Grafton, Hall, and Polydore Vergil, through numerous fifteenth-century records like those of Fabyan, Gregory, Hardyng, Thomas of Walsingham, and the chronicle of *Brut,* and through earlier compilations like those of

Ranulph Higden, Matthew Paris, Giraldus Cambrensis, Geoffrey of Monmouth, the *Anglo-Saxon Chronicle,* and Bede's *Ecclesiastical History.* Now and then attempts were made to weed this immense accumulation of fact and legend from the more obvious exotics, but in general, by the 1570's, when Raphael Holinshed headed the syndicate of scholars which put together the most famous of Tudor histories, the record contained much good history and also many stimulating romantifications to set at work a poet's imagination—in *Shakespeare's Workmanship* Sir Arthur Quiller-Couch suggests how Shakespeare's dramatic nerves must have twitched when, leafing through Holinshed's *History of Scotland,* he came on the three women in strange and ferly apparel who foretold the future and who were to play so remarkable a part in *Macbeth.* Professor Dover Wilson has written of history as being in the sixteenth century "a recent discovery," and so in a sense it was; but in substance it was an abundant store of events, legends, and moralizings.

As for its *volume,* as well as its antiquity, that cannot fail to strike the observer, from the mid-fifteenth century onward; with this aspect of the matter Professor Lily Campbell and Dr. Wright have dealt particularly well. Increasingly there is a hunger for history; intellectual activity shifts outside the monasteries to the lay world, to lawyers and men of affairs; more and more chronicles are compiled; and toward 1500 the printing press begins its momentous campaign of popularization. Caxton printed *The Chronicles of England* in 1480 and Trevisa's translation of Higden's *Polychronicon* in 1482; to the latter he prefixed (as both earlier and later historians were wont to do) a sonorous prologue celebrating the virtues of histori-

cal studies. Noting *en passant* the appearance of Malory's
Morte d'Arthur in 1485, Lydgate's *Fall of Princes* in 1494
(which in 1559 prompted a continuation, deeply important for Elizabethan drama, as *A Mirror for Magistrates*),
Richard Arnold's *Chronicle* in 1502 and Fabyan's in 1516,
we arrive at the fruitful early decades of the sixteenth century. At Henry VIII's command Lord Berners in 1523–
1525 published his great translation of Froissart, and about
1513 Sir Thomas More wrote that wonderful life of Richard III which, published in Hardyng's *Chronicle* in 1543,
taken over by Hall and Holinshed and thence by Shakespeare, has remained the classic portrait of Crookback, a
travesty though Richard's supporters protest it to be.

Concurrently, the main formative event of Tudor historiography was taking place: encouraged successively by
Henry VII and Henry VIII, Polydore Vergil, Italian hu-
manist and scholar, who had arrived in England about
1502, was writing his history of England, the *Anglica historia*. This was printed in Latin at Basel in 1534; it went
through many Continental editions, though none appeared until the nineteenth century in England; English
historians drew upon it and learnt from it. Hall and others
often translate it, and Miss Lily Campbell calls Vergil's appointment "for English historiography the most important event of the reign of Henry VII." His most recent
editor, Denys Hay, has stressed his importance as follows:

From Vergil, Hall derived three fundamental notions; history
is the record of the past in a form designed to perpetuate fame
and glory; it is "memory by literature"; it must nevertheless
be based on a critical use of sources; it must have an argument.

One of these notions—the perpetuation of fame—derived
from many older sources, particularly from Cicero, Pliny

93

the Younger, or Tacitus; the second, the critical use of sources, led Vergil to disparage the revered legends of King Arthur and of Brutus as the founding father of Britain; the third was fruitful in method, the interpretation of history as theme or argument instead of its mere recording as annals of events. As adopted by Hall, this bore importantly on the writing of history in England and on history as Shakespeare received it and consequently handled it.

So the writing and printing of histories was a major preoccupation of Tudor scholarship and the reading of histories one of the strongest cultural phenomena of the age—histories of all times and places, of a single reign, of foreign countries, translated from classical or Continental sources, in prose, in verse, in drama. As Professor Haller remarks, "The primary enterprise of writers and publishers of books . . . was to get the literature and accumulated knowledge of past ages transposed into English and put into print." [1] "Right courteous Gentlemen," begins the preface to the Herodotus translated in 1584 by B. R. (possibly Barnabe Rich):

We have brought out of Greece into England two of the Muses, Clio and Euterpe, as desirous to see the land as to learn the language; whom I trust you will use well because they be women, and you can not abuse them because you be gentlemen.*

Clio and Euterpe, History and Music, are here the names of the two books of Herodotus which B. R. translates, but the meaning can be generalized: history is a growing passion, aspiring to the status of an art.

---

* This, and all subsequent quotations, have been modernized by the editor.

[1] *Foxe's Book of Martyrs and the Elect Nation* (London, 1963), p. 134.

It has been said that a volume could be filled with praises of history from the prefaces of Renaissance historians. Here is Caxton, in the *Polychronicon* of 1482:

> Great thankings, laud, and honor we meritoriously ben bound to yield and offer unto writers of histories, which greatly have profited our mortal life, that show unto the readers and hearers by the ensamples of things past what thing is to be desired and what is to be eschewed.

"The fruits of virtue ben immortal," Caxton asserts, "specially when they ben wrapped in the benefice of histories." "The end of all histories," declares Thomas Bedingfield, prefacing his translation of Machiavelli's *Florentine History* in 1588 (pub. 1595), "ought to be to move men unto virtue and discourage them from vice." Actually, Bede had said the same thing 750 years earlier, dedicating to King Ceolwulf his own great history:

> If history records good things of good men, the thoughtful hearer is encouraged to imitate what is good; or if it records evil of wicked ones, the good religious listener is encouraged to avoid all that is sinful and perverse.

And, indeed, centuries before Bede himself, Tacitus had said the same thing. But to return to the sixteenth century, here is Alexander Barclay when he translates Sallust's *Jugurtha* about 1520:

> Great is the laud and many be the commodities and utilities of histories. An history is the recorder of times past: the light of verity: the maistresse of man's living, the precedent of memory, the messenger of antiquity. And (as Titus Livius recordeth in his prologue) the knowledge of histories among other things is most wholesome, necessary, and profitable.

But that again is not original; Barclay was repeating Cicero's words in *De oratore,* which call history the witness of times, light of truth, life of memory, mistress of life, and messenger of antiquity. And after later echoes than Barclay's the Latin manifesto is splendidly emblemized in 1614 on the title page of Raleigh's *History of the World:* here, in the great engraving, History as *Magistra Vitae,* flanked by Experience and Truth, stands sustaining the globe and trampling on Death and Oblivion, between classical columns labeled with Cicero's phrases. Hardyng's *Chronicle,* published by Richard Grafton in 1543, has a preface praising history as shaming vice, immortalizing virtue, and recording the fates of kingdoms. These are ideas the Tudors never weary of reciting: Hall's great *Union of the Two Noble and Illustrate Families of Lancaster and York* (1548) does so with exceptional rhetoric:

> Thus, writing is the key to induce virtue and repress vice. Thus memory maketh men dead many a thousand year still to live as though they were present. Thus Fame triumpheth upon Death and renown upon Oblivion, and all by reason of writing and history.

So, popular, belauded, self-consciously important, preluded with drum rolls and sounding brass of sonorous prose, the Tudor historians trundle forward their folios and quartos as majestically, as irresistibly, as ponderously indeed, as Hannibal's elephants. But how did history acquire the sense of color, drama, excitement, which made it a promising source for the dramatist? Let us consider now how it acquired not prestige but literary or dramatic virtues.

Literary or dramatic virtues are not easy to find in the very early chronicles, though this general admission is not meant to cover Bede's *Ecclesiastical History;* Bede is a writer of noble quality and his book still lives nobly. But Bede is much too early for the present purpose; nearly a millennium was to pass before Shakespeare was born, and though, like the other early British historians Gildas and Nennius, Bede was drawn upon by later chroniclers, much had to happen before Shakespeare's time in the writing of history. Much less of a work of art is the ninth-century *Anglo-Saxon Chronicle;* this is interesting in detail, but an annual record can hardly have a theme or unity. There is more promise in Matthew Paris' thirteenth-century *English History*, the *Historia Anglorum*. This can be colorful and high-spirited (opinionated, indeed); it can set forth scenes and ceremonials and tell with feeling such a story as that of little St. Hugh of Lincoln, a version of which Chaucer was to use for his *Prioress' Tale*. Matthew Paris was praised by some of the more scholarly Tudors as one of the few useful medievalists; so too was Thomas of Walsingham, contemporary with Richard II, Henry IV, and Henry V, whose *Historia Anglicana* covers with care the ground which Shakespeare was to occupy, though Shakespeare's direct sources are much later. Yet here again, there is little of a literary savor in Thomas of Walsingham, little of emotion or characterization or contemplation. Facts are there, color is not. Color and emotion are qualities rather of the French chronicles which deal with the fall of Richard II, and particularly are they evident in Froissart; but Froissart does not become important in England until Lord Berners had published his translation in 1523, and then his splendor and passion make their contribution to the Tudor world and, indeed, some scholars believe, directly to Shakespeare. The only native medievalist who is a major influence on Elizabethan historiography and historical drama is Geoffrey of Monmouth in the early twelfth century. Geoffrey was very influential indeed, though influential for his legends rather than his history. According to his account, an ancient Welsh manuscript came into his hands, relating the pre-Roman history of Britain, which Bede and Gildas had not known, and he translated it from the original into Latin. As with Macpherson and Ossian in the eighteenth century, it is not clear whence he really derived his material, but his importance lies in the result, all that wonderful fable and legend which, until the skeptical Restoration, held in thrall the imagination of British patriots: the stories about Britain's early colonization by Brutus, great-grandson of Aeneas, the founder of Troynovant or London, and of the naming of England, Scotland, and Wales—Loegria, Albania, and Cambria—after his three sons, Locrine, Albanact, and Camber; the stories too about Uther Pendragon, King Arthur, and Merlin. These groups of legends, those of Brutus and those of Arthur, are sown broadcast into Elizabethan literature. The first produces that strange genealogy of kings which so fascinated Elizabethan poets and playwrights—Brutus, Locrine, Bladud the founder of Bath, his son Leir of Leicester, and Leir's three daughters; later on Gorboduc with his sons, Ferrex and Porrex; and later again Cymbeline with his sons, Guiderius and Arviragus. Here too is Old King Cole, of Colchester. The second legend, the Arthurian, relates the prophecies of Merlin, the reigns of Uther Pendragon and King Arthur, the wounding of Arthur in battle with Modred, and his being taken to die in the Lake Isle of Avalon.

A long dispute arose as to whether these stories were true or not. Geoffrey of Monmouth was not the only source of them: Arthurian legends are widespread in France and Britain. In the sixteenth and seventeenth centuries there was a battle of the books about the whole matter not less fierce, and lasting far longer, than that about the Ancients and the Moderns in the later seventeenth century. Conflicting historians raged furiously together. Polydore Vergil was scornful: against him patriots and antiquarians like Bale, Leland, and Foxe could not bring themselves to give up this flattering prehistory, this rich romance of Romano-British legend.[2] Spenser wrote a whole canto of *The Faerie Queene* specifically upon it; Ben Jonson told Drummond of Hawthornden that "for a heroic poem there was no such ground as King Arthur's fiction"; Milton and Dryden contemplated Arthurian epics; and an Elizabethan club including Richard Mulcaster, the famous schoolmaster of Merchant Taylors', formed itself into "The Ancient Order, Society, and Unity Laudable of Prince Arthur and His Knightly Armory of the Round Table," whose members adopted the names of knights in the *Morte d'Arthur* and assembled at Mile End Green in London for the encouragement of archery and military prowess. Justice Shallow, it may be recalled, boasted of having in his youth been Sir Dagonet in

[2] The whole Brutus story was scathingly dismissed in George Buchanan's *Rerum Scoticorum historia* (1582) as an "impudentissim[um] mendaci[um]" (fol. 15r) and Geoffrey as "Monachus ille hujus Brutinae fabulae poeta" (i.e., fabricator; fol. 16r). A rejoinder came from Richard Harvey, Gabriel Harvey's brother, entitled *Philadelphus, or, A Defense of Brutus and the Brutans' History* (1593), which stoutly defended Geoffrey of Monmouth and declared that "neither seven Polydores more, nor ten Buchanans, shall persuade me that this genealogy is a fabulous tale. Let Polydore get him to Urbin in Italy and Buchanan hie him to Buchany in Scotland: it becometh not these outlandish intruders to usurp the censure of the Brutan histories" (p. 17). For the Harvey reference I am indebted to Mr. John Crow.

Arthur's show—Sir Dagonet, appropriately, was Arthur's Fool. It was, indeed, part of Tudor propaganda to stress the supposed descent of Henry VII from the line of Arthur, and Arthur was the name given to Henry's eldest son, who, however, died young. How, one wonders, would English history have gone had we had a King Arthur instead of Henry VIII?

Fortunately Holinshed's chronicles were not so skeptical as to reject all these and other legends of prehistory—or the world would lack *King Lear* and *Cymbeline* and (from Scottish sources) *Macbeth.*

Yet though legend may start with imaginative advantages, real history gradually acquired emotional potency and a sense of dramatic characterization. In particular, the tragedy of Richard II focused a deep charge of feeling. When in the *Brut,* that fifteenth-century chronicle whose popularity is attested by its survival in well over a hundred manuscript copies, we read the following comment on the tragedy of Richard, we have the germ of Shakespeare's emotion in his play:

All the good hearts of the realm clean turned away from him ever after, and that was utterly destruction and end of him that was so high and so excellent a king, through covetise and false counsel. Alas for pity, that such a king might not see! [*The Brut,* ed. F. W. Brie, II (1908), 356.]

And whatever may be said about the undeveloped state of early historiography, when we come upon a passage like the following, on Richard's last moments, we are clearly in the presence of someone who can write with power and effect—this also is from the *Brut:*

Anon commanded Sir Piers of Exton that he should go straight to Pomfret and deliver the world of King Richard. And so he departed from the King and went to the castle of Pomfret, whereas King Richard was in prison, the which was set at table for to dine. And anon after Sir Piers came into the chamber where the King was and eight men with him, and each man an ax in his hand. Truth it is that when the King saw Sir Piers with his fellowship enter into the chamber defensibly arrayed, he shoved the table from him and sprang in the midst of them and caught an ax out of one of their hands and set him valiantly at defense. And, himself defending, he slew four of the eight. And when the said Sir Piers saw the King so defend him, he was sore abashed and greatly afeard and forthwith started upon the place whereas King Richard was wont to sit. And as King Richard fought and defended himself, going backward, the said Sir Piers smote him on the head grievously with an ax, that he fell to the ground. Then cried King Richard, "God, mercy!" And then he gave him yet another great stroke on the head. And so he died anon. And thus was this noble king slain and murdered. [Text from Higden, *Polychronicon,* 1527, fol. cccxxv, cap. ix.]

The date of that is about 1480, and after being printed in the *Polychronicon* it appeared, somewhat paraphrased, in Hall's *Chronicle,* and then in Holinshed's, and so came under Shakespeare's eyes.

By 1500, historical narrative could manage some fine scenes, some emotion and eloquence. But shape, pattern, theme, these are hardly to be discovered. The next fifty years produced Berners' translation of Froissart, Polydore Vergil's *Anglica historia,* More's *Richard III,* and Hall's *Chronicle* of the houses of Lancaster and York. There is no reason why Shakespeare should not have read Froissart, and it is often assumed he did so—Professor Dover Wilson thinks he detects borrowings. I do not think that the evidence amounts to proof: yet certainly Froissart's John of Gaunt, lamenting on his deathbed over Richard's misrule, is, in manner and substance, much like Shakespeare's. Froissart's treatment of Richard's downfall, in any case, ex-

Arthur R. Humphreys

hibits great quality in its writing. History here may well be reckoned a "new discovery": there is a dramatic sense of events trending in one fatal direction over a long period; there is a high expectancy, as an explosive situation is felt in the making; there is brilliant color and life, in the description of Richard's lavish household, his jousts at Windsor, and Henry IV's coronation. There are memorable characterizations, living dialogue, and a sense of the swarming life of the nation behind the protagonists. Froissart writes beautifully, and Berners translates him worthily. Here is Richard's deposition speech, and, though Shakespeare greatly outgoes it, it has a poignancy which deeply humanizes history:

Cousin of Lancaster, I regard and consider mine estate, which is as now but small, I thank God thereof. As any more to reign or to govern people, or to bear a crown, I think it not; and, as God help me, I would I were dead by a natural death and that the French king had again his daughter. We have had as yet no great joy together, nor sith I brought her to England I could never have the love of my people as I had before. Cousin, all things considered, I know well I have greatly trespassed against you and against other noblemen of my blood; by divers things, I perceive I shall never have pardon nor come to peace; wherefore, with mine own free and liberal will, I will resign to you the heritage of the crown of England, and I require you to take the gift thereof with the resignation.

In date of publication Berners' Froissart is the first history in English to be great literature. But in date of composition it was preceded by More's *History of Richard III*, not published until Grafton included it thirty years later in Hardyng's *Chronicle* in 1543. Shortly after it was published, Roger Ascham praised it as a model of what such things should be:

102

Shakespeare and Tudor History

Sir Thomas More, in that pamphlet of Richard the Third, doth in most part, I believe, of all these points so content men, as, if the rest of our story of England were so done, we might well compare with France, Italy, or Germany in that behalf. [*A Report . . . on the Affairs and State of Germany,* written ca. 1552, pub. ca. 1570, A iiijr.]

Through More, via Shakespeare, this short reign of two years, ending with that defeat in 1485 on Bosworth Field which we take to mark, if any event can, the end of the Middle Ages, has stamped itself ineffaceably on the imagination of English-speaking people. More's *History* did for Shakespeare in this instance what Plutarch's *Lives* did in others: it presented a striking life story which gave shape and significance to a train of events. The portrait of Richard is unforgettable:

[He was] little of stature, ill-featured of limbs, crookbacked, the left shoulder much higher than his right, hard-favored of visage, and such as is in states [noblemen] called warlike, in other men otherwise. He was malicious, wrathful, envious, and from afore his birth ever froward. It is for truth reported that the Duchess, his mother, had so much ado in her travail that she could not be delivered of him uncut; and that he came into the world with the feet forward, . . . and (as the fame runneth), also not untoothed. . . . He was close and secret, a deep dissimuler, lowly of countenance, arrogant of heart, outwardly coumpinable [companionable] where he inwardly hated, not letting [omitting] to kiss whom he thought to kill, despitious and cruel, not for evil will alway, but often for ambition. . . . Friend and foe was muchwhat indifferent; where his advantage grew, he spared no man's death whose life withstood his purpose.

After he had killed the young Princes, writes More,

he never had quiet in his mind; he never thought himself sure. Where he went abroad, his eyen whirled about, his

body privily fenced, his hand ever on his dagger, his countenance and manner like one alway ready to strike again. He
took ill rest a-nights, lay long waking and musing, sore
wearied with care and watch, rather slumbered than slept,
troubled with fearful dreams, sometime start up, leap out of
his bed, and run about the chamber, so was his restless heart
continually tossed and tumbled.

And to complete the portrait:

The while he was thinking of any matter, he did continually
bite his nether lip, as though that cruel nature of his did so
rage against itself in that little carcass. Also he was wont to be
ever with his right hand pulling out the sheath to the midst
and putting in again the dagger which he did alway wear.
Truly, he had a sharp wit, provident and subtle, apt both to
counterfeit and dissemble; his courage also haught and fierce,
which failed him not in the very death, which, when his men
forsook him, he rather yielded to take with the sword than by
foul flight to prolong his life. [Text taken from *The Complete
Works of St. Thomas More*, II, *Richard III,* ed. R. S. Sylvester
(1963), 7–8, 87, and *Three Books of Polydore Vergil's English
History,* ed. H. Ellis (1844), p. 277. Hardyng, Hall, and
Holinshed have very similar accounts.]

The first half of that is from More, the second half from
the translation of Polydore Vergil's history which Grafton
used to complete More's incomplete story: but whatever
the source it makes fascinating historical reading, a perfect
prompting for a dramatist's mind. How indeed could a
dramatist resist such a portrait, such a psychology? Shakespeare takes the note perfectly and opens his play with
masterful assurance. After a few lines of Marlovian gran-
diloquence but more than Marlovian expressiveness he
realizes in the fullest poetic amplitude all that More has
given of Richard's sinister power, together with a vivifying
brilliance of glee, bitterness, and ironical wit. Each word
exerts a graphic particular force, sound and syntax playing

together in that organic spiritedness we only really expect from Shakespeare's full maturity, the whole complex of attitudes and tones being achieved in terms which give the actor every opportunity of embodying them in gesture and nuance:

> Now is the winter of our discontent
> Made glorious summer by this sun of York;
> And all the clouds that lour'd upon our house
> In the deep bosom of the ocean buried.
> Now are our brows bound with victorious wreaths;
> Our bruised arms hung up for monuments;
> Our stern alarums chang'd to merry meetings;
> Our dreadful marches to delightful measures.
> Grim-visag'd War hath smooth'd his wrinkled front;
> And now, instead of mounting barbed steeds,
> To fright the souls of fearful adversaries,
> He capers nimbly in a lady's chamber
> To the lascivious pleasing of a lute.
> But I, that am not shap'd for sportive tricks,
> Nor made to court an amorous looking-glass;
> I, that am rudely stamp'd, and want love's majesty,
> To strut before a wanton ambling nymph;
> I, that am curtail'd of this fair proportion,
> Cheated of feature by dissembling Nature,
> Deform'd, unfinish'd, sent before my time
> Into this breathing world scarce half made up,
> And that so lamely and unfashionable
> That dogs bark at me as I halt by them;
> Why, I, in this weak piping time of peace,
> Have no delight to pass away the time,
> Unless to spy my shadow in the sun
> And descant on mine own deformity.
> And therefore, since I cannot prove a lover,
> To entertain these fair well-spoken days,
> I am determined to prove a villain.

This, one of the greatest things Shakespeare ever did, is the passage Thomas Gray chose to demonstrate to his friend

West that "Shakespeare's language is one of his principal beauties. . . . Every word in him is a picture," and that since Shakespeare's time dramatic style had "greatly degenerated." [3] More's was an incisive and striking prose portrait: Shakespeare's is a full imaginative realization of a human being, alive in every movement of the verse. Still, as often in his uses of sources, the excellence of his original has clearly stimulated him to a brilliant result. It may be historically unjust that More portrayed Richard as he did, but that it was dramatically fortunate all but the most devoted supporters of the King must surely agree.

By the time More's and Polydore Vergil's work was at all widely disseminated, sixteenth-century historical writing was virtually established as a major achievement. The seminal importance of Polydore Vergil's work has been amply established in recent decades: Grafton's continuation in 1543 of Hardyng's *Chronicle* draws freely upon him, so does Hall's and Grafton's own *Chronicle* of 1563, and Stow's, and Holinshed's. He interpreted the personalities of the Wars of the Roses in ways which enhanced the prestige of the Lancastrians (he was, after all, commissioned to write his history by Henry VII), and his portraits, via the chroniclers and Shakespeare, have become as much a part of the national inheritance as has Richard Crookback—the saintly Henry VI, intriguing Suffolk and Margaret of Anjou, prudent Henry VII, noble Catherine of Aragon, and overweening Wolsey (Polydore did not like Wolsey at all). He saw history as organized narrative in the fashion of Plutarch and other classical historians. Much of this passes into Hall's chronicle of 1548, the *Union of the Two Noble and Illustrate Families of Lan-*

[3] *Letters,* April, Thursday [1742].

caster and York. This begins its account where Shakespeare was to begin, with the Mowbray-Bolingbroke
quarrel under Richard II, and ends where Shakespeare's
sequence was to end, with the union of the houses under
Henry Richmond of Lancaster and Elizabeth of York. In
this pattern each reign has a title marking its specific
character, though the page-by-page conduct of the narrative is less differentiated than the titles: "The unquiet
time of King Henry the Fourth," "The victorious acts of
King Henry the Vth," "The troublous season of King
Henry the VI," and so on, up to "The politic governance
of King Henry the VII" and "The triumphant reign of
King Henry the VIII." I believe Professor Geoffrey
Bullough is right in doubting whether Shakespeare drew
from Hall much more than the moral scheme and general
shape of his successive reigns; certainly his debts are primarily to Holinshed. Still, Hall does give form to the curve
of events over eight reigns, he underlines morals, and he
heightens the contrasts of fate. C. L. Kingsford's *English
Historical Literature in the Fifteenth Century* (1913)
long ago pointed out Hall's importance in perceiving the
shape underlying the confusions of fifteenth-century history:

That Hall grasped [the unity and importance of fifteenth-
century history] is shown by the title he gave to his chonicle.
It appears also in the continuous cycle of Shakespeare's histories. The downfall of Richard II, the glories of Henry V, the
long struggle of Lancaster and York, ending in the happy
union of the rival houses, were all stages in the preparation
for a greater age.

Hall's theme became "the Tudor myth." Hall is one of the
main sources, and is accepted in cases of discrepancy as the
guiding authority, for the compilers of the *Mirror for*

Arthur R. Humphreys

Magistrates of 1559, that sequence of verse biographies which stresses the moral dramas of statesmen's fates. When Sir Thomas Wyatt the younger was on the scaffold, to be executed for his part in the rebellion of 1554, he delivered a confession and repentance for his act, instancing the course of events which had been Hall's theme: here is his speech as Grafton's chronicle of 1563 gives it:

Peruse the Chronicles through, and you shall see that never rebellion attempted by subjects against their prince and country from the beginning did ever prosper or had better success, except the case of King Henry the Fourth, who although he became a prince, yet in his act was but a rebel, for so must I call him. And though he prevailed for a time, yet was it not long, but that his heirs were deprived and those that had right again restored to the kingdom and crown, and the usurpation so sharply revenged afterward in his blood as it well appeared that the long delay of God's vengeance was supplied with more grievous plague in the third and fourth generation. For the love of God, all you gentlemen that be here present, remember and be taught as well by examples past as also by this my present infelicity and most wretched case. [Grafton, *Chronicle* (1563), pp. 1339–1340, quoted in *Mirror for Magistrates* (1938), pp. 49–50.]

The great theme of due succession broken in the fall of Richard, and of national harmony restored only with the accession of Henry Tudor, was not solely Hall's invention: Roger Ascham's *Toxophilus,* which came out in 1545 and was dedicated to Henry VIII, includes the recognized doctrine that Henry's father had blessedly healed a shattered realm:

The bloody civil war of England betwixt the house of York and Lancaster, where shafts flew of both sides, to the destruction of many a yeoman of England whom foreign battle could never have subdued, both I will pass over for the pitifulness of it and yet may we highly praise God in the remembrance of it, seeing he of his providence hath so knit together those two noble houses with so noble and pleasant a flower. [1545, p. 40r.]

Yet Hall achieved the grand formulation of the doctrine, and Shakespeare gave it permanence.

One other quality in Hall should be mentioned, his reading of history much in terms of personal character and conduct. Denys Hay has argued that Polydore Vergil would have disapproved the practice whereby Tudor historians like Hall see history in terms of character. Yet this quality, in More, Hall, Holinshed, and the poet Samuel Daniel (on whom Shakespeare certainly drew), is above all one a dramatist would value: it is in the play of personalities, especially as they center on royal courts, that myth and history have always offered the richest field for the imagination. And though the economic interpretation of history is no doubt the right one for our own *Zeitgeist,* the personal interpretation is the one most encouraging to drama, the one most encouraging, perhaps, to the human spirit.

I must digress a moment from the Tudor historians one can see as directly or indirectly behind Shakespeare to one whom one cannot (except, it may be, in a detail or two),[4] but whose importance in his own way is second to none. Foxe's *Acts and Monuments* (1563, enlarged in 1570) must certainly be reckoned among the most remarkable of Elizabethan historical compilations. The general reader of today will, I suspect, look on much of Foxe's great work as a load of learned lumber, though sometimes inflammatory

[4] Mr. E. A. J. Honigmann, in his revised Arden edition of *King John,* points to small common features between Foxe's account of John and Shakespeare's, but these may well be accidental.

lumber; innumerable martyrdoms narrated in clichés of praise or obloquy and varied by interminable theological disputations are hardly to the modern taste. Yet, as Professor Haller points out, under the apparently endless accumulation of instances there lies the great scheme of a universal church history of the true faith in which, while leaving to the chroniclers the facts of lay history, Foxe sought to show the supreme position of Elizabeth and her people as the rescuers and guardians of Christian belief. Though the execution of this theme is often obscured, the vision is rather like that by which Milton, in the fervor of a renovating faith, saw "a noble and puissant nation rousing herself like a strong man after sleep, and shaking her invincible locks" (*Areopagitica*). Moreover, Foxe planted in the memory of his innumerable readers—and indeed of those who do not read him—many a cherished story, like that of Queen Mary on her deathbed saying, "When I am dead and opened, you shall find Calais lying on my heart." The *Acts and Monuments*, at its best, rates impressively as history and literature together, when, for example, it relates the interrogation of Lady Jane Grey, or the examination of Ridley; or when it tells most excellently the life of Cranmer, up to the famous incident of his holding out his offending hand to be burnt; or when it gives the unforgettable account of the execution of Latimer and Ridley. Episodes like these do, in Latimer's great words (whether his actual words, or a wonderful later invention), "light such a candle by God's grace in England as I trust shall never be put out." As Professor Haller remarks,

One can only marvel, here as at other points of Foxe's book, at the unfailing gift which all sorts of English people in that time seem to have had at command for appropriate, expressive, and dramatic speech.

Latimer's famous utterance is, I may add, followed by an account of Ridley's sufferings as he burns which is, I think, the most dreadful rendering of the horrible I have ever read; there were Tudor horrors as well as Tudor glories. For three centuries Foxe's text and its woodcuts, progressively vulgarized and sensationalized, fixed in the Anglo-Saxon mind the most alarming notions of Roman Catholicism (notions not yet wholly extinct); his effects have indeed been powerful, and to speak about the Tudor historians is necessarily to reckon with him. But Shakespeare seems to have been virtually or wholly untouched by him.

As for other historians who did touch him, Stow with his *Annals* of 1592, and pre-eminently Holinshed with the *Chronicles* of 1577 and 1587, their contribution to the art of historical writing is less original than More's or Froissart's or Polydore's or Hall's, though Stow's scholarship is admirable, the sweep of Holinshed's vast narrative is grand, and their contribution to the plays' contents is overwhelmingly important. They write interesting prose, they have an energetic spirit which keeps their narratives moving and a good sense of animated character, and in many a passage of moralizing they invest their stories with a popular emotion which Shakespeare was further to enrich. Holinshed in particular provides God's plenty, broad in sweep, ample in detail, entertaining by rumors, superstitions, and anecdotes, assembling into a magnificent compendious whole the work of his precursors, and by this very inclusiveness furnishing to Shakespeare an absorbing miscellany through which his keen eye picked its selective way. No one who studies Shakespeare's relevance and economy, when he translates his miscellaneous originals into dramatic form, eliciting living rhythms and organic shapes from the jumble of oddments, heightening interesting but confused traits into gripping and full characterizations, combining into a connected interplaying whole his material from different quarters—no one who does this can be anything but awed at the constructive intelligence he displays. Out of interesting but ill-shaped and often uncritical assemblages of facts and comments, far too abundant for the less-than-three-hours' traffic of the stage, he selects, refines, sharpens, counterpoints, combines, so that the action is a clear strong narrative of human purposes. Coleridge offers the appropriate comment in his *Literary Remains:*

> He had unequivocally proved the indwelling in his mind of imagination, or the power by which one image or feeling is made to modify many others, and by a sort of fusion to force many into one;—that which afterwards showed itself in such might and energy in *Lear,* where the deep anguish of a father spreads the feeling of ingratitude and cruelty over the very elements of heaven;—and which, combining many circumstances into one moment of consciousness, tends to produce that ultimate end of all human thought and feeling, unity.

It is the unity elicited out of the great heaps of chronicle history that is the structural measure, as it is the rich characterization that is the psychological measure, and the vivid style the poetical measure, of Shakespeare's superiority over his sources. But his historians were not unworthy of him: through many years they had put together the great story of the past with energy, scholarship, and increasing art, so that history should indeed be the mistress of life, messenger of antiquity, light of truth, life of memory, and witness of times.

Shakespeare in Czechoslovakia*

By ZDENĚK STŘÍBRNÝ

THE story of Shakespeare in Czechoslovakia is a long one
and I cannot expect you to listen for too long a time to the
parade of Czech and Slovak Shakespearean translators,
critics, scholars, actors, producers, and other artists and en-
thusiasts whose names are bound to sound strange and far-
off to you. Therefore, I shall try to concentrate only on the
most important periods and events. Even so, I hope that
Shakespeare's humanizing impact in the cultural life of
Central Europe will emerge clearly enough.

The poet himself must have thought of my country as an
exotic place. If we were to take the make-believe of *The
Winter's Tale* quite literally, we should envisage him im-
agining his "fair Bohemia" as a remote land, lashed by rag-
ing seas and "famous for the creatures / Of prey." [1] We

* Delivered on September 20, 1964. Mr. Stříbrný is a professor
of English and American literature at Charles University, Prague.
[1] *The Winter's Tale*, IV.i.21; III.iii.12–13. Quotations from Shake-

realize, however, that for him, as for other Elizabethan popular writers, the maritime Bohemia was just a fairyland of a winter's tale, a Renaissance pastoral, and so were her shepherds, singing and ale-drinking pickpockets, exposed children growing into damsels in distress, lovelorn princes, and angry old kings.

Yet not to suppress any trace of plain evidence, I should admit that Shakespeare's other references to my country or countrymen are still more ambiguous and less flattering. In *Twelfth Night*, Feste, in one of his clowning fits of clever nonsense, speaks of "the old hermit of Prague, that never saw pen and ink" and who "very wittily said to a niece of King Gorboduc, 'That that is is.' " [2] Despite many attempts of historians and critics alike, the puzzling Prague hermit has successfully escaped any definite identification (the same is true of the equally puzzling niece of King Gorboduc). And I suspect that that is exactly what Shakespeare wanted: to sharpen our wits and incense our fantasy by problems both great and small, serious and funny.

Nor can we make head or tail of mine host of the Garter in *The Merry Wives of Windsor* when he jibes at the boorish servant Peter Simple, calling him a "Bohemian Tartar"—a truly fantastic breed! [3] Finally, the Bohemian-born prisoner, Barnardine, in *Measure for Measure*, drunk and rebellious, is also a rather enigmatic type of a sturdy Elizabethan beatnik.[4]

For all that, Shakespeare's own work has met with a

---

speare are from the "Globe Edition" by W. G. Clark and W. A. Wright (London, 1864, and later).

[2] *Twelfth Night*, IV.ii.14–17.

[3] *The Merry Wives of Windsor*, IV.v.21.

[4] See *Measure for Measure*, IV.iii.22 ff.

warm reception in my country from the very beginning. It is exciting to suppose—and there are reasons for doing so—that his plays were performed in Bohemia and Moravia by strolling English and German players even during his lifetime and certainly shortly after his death. At the turn of the sixteenth century Prague was the seat of the Emperor Rudolf II and, accordingly, an important political and cultural center which maintained lively relations with the England of Elizabeth I and James I. Among the visitors to London was a Moravian nobleman, Zdeněk Brtnický of Wallenstein, who in 1600 recorded in his Latin diary two visits to a public theater at the Bankside—possibly the newly erected Globe, where Shakespeare's greatest plays were produced. The young traveler did not comment on the plays he had seen (probably he could hardly follow them), but he gives us his description of the theater building, which deserves to be quoted:

On Monday, 3rd July.

We heard an English comedy: the theater is built of wood in the manner of the ancient Romans and so shaped that the spectators can see every detail quite comfortably from all parts. On our return we crossed a bridge adorned with magnificent buildings, and fixed on one of these there are still to be seen the heads of some earls and noblemen who were convicted of treason and executed.[5]

---

[5] The original Latin text is as follows: *Die* ☽ *[Lunae]. 3. Julii. Audivimus comoediam Anglicam: theatrum ad morem antiquorum Romanorum constructum ex lignis, ita formatum ut omnibus ex partibus spectatores commodissime singula videre possint. In reditu transivimus pontem magnificis aedificiis ornatum, e quibus uni adhuc affixa cernuntur capita quorundam comitum et nobilium, qui laesae Majestatis rei supplicio affecti sunt.* I quote from a copy kept at the State Central Archives in Prague, Manuscript collection B 21: Diarium Zdenkonis de Waldstein. The original can be found

Zdeněk Stříbrný

I believe that this little piece of evidence, however brief and sadly inaccurate, might be of interest to American scholars who have made such a distinguished contribution to the study of the Elizabethan and Jacobean stage. The mention of the classical Roman model, in particular, gives a new hint for further discussion. Certainly the description agrees with and slightly adds to the better-known account of another Central European visitor to London, Dr. Thomas Platter of Basel, who also went twice to a London theater, the first time to see *Julius Caesar,* at the Globe, too, as it seems, on September 21, 1599.

On the other hand, it is recorded that a company of English strolling actors, led by John Greene, visited Moravia in 1617 and went to Prague in the same year to take part in the coronation festivities of the Hapsburg King Ferdinand II of Styria. A rival company of Protestant affiliation, directed by Robert Browne, played in Prague in 1619–1620 for Frederick the Elector Palatine, who was crowned King by the Czech estates in protest against the Hapsburgs. Frederick and his English wife, Elizabeth, daughter of James I, were both patrons of actors. During their marriage celebrations in London in 1613 a number

---

in the Vatican Library in Rome, dept. Regina Sueciae, Lat. 666. The given passage was known to E. K. Chambers, as seen from *The Elizabethan Stage* (Oxford, 1923), II, 366, where it is quoted in the Latin original after C. A. Mills, who published it in the *Times,* April 11, 1914, denoting his source rather vaguely as the travels of "a foreign nobleman, to be published by J. A. F. Orbaan from a Vatican MS." The Vatican original was pointed out by B. Dudík in *Iter Romanum* (Vienna, 1855), I, 232–244. Cf. O. Odložilík, "Cesty z Čech a Moravy do Velké Británie v letech 1563–1620," *Časopis Matice moravské,* LIX (1935), 241–320; O. Vočadlo, "Český Shakespeare," preface and notes to the complete re-edition of Shakespeare's works in Czech, I (Prague, 1959), 5–6 and 583.

of plays were produced, almost one half of them by Shake-speare, including *The Winter's Tale*.[6] Therefore, it is per-haps not too fanciful to say that Frederick's rule in the Czech lands might have brought about an early flowering of a genuine Shakespearean drama on the European conti-nent. Unfortunately, the speedy overthrow of the Protes-tant armies at the battle of the White Mountain near Prague by the end of 1620 forced Frederick, the "Winter King," hastily to leave Bohemia and thus for a long time to bury Czech hopes of an independent political and cultural life.

Instead, a severe Counter Reformation and Germaniza-tion of the Czech lands by the Hapsburg dynasty set in, ag-gravated by the horrors of the Thirty Years' War. Many Czechs emigrated to Western Europe to seek religious free-dom or better fortune. Among them was the etcher Wenceslaus Hollar (1607–1677), whose many engravings of London are rounded off by the "Long View," clearly showing the shape and even a part of the interior of the sec-ond Globe.

Despite all the difficulties, more strolling actors were coming to Bohemia. Shortly after the Thirty Years' War, in 1651, a German group from Dresden was permitted to visit Prague with a repertory including *Julius Caesar* and a very garbled version of *The Merchant of Venice*. In 1658 *Romeo and Juliet* was played by English actors at a ban-quet of the Prague high society. One of the spectators, the Archbishop of Prague, Cardinal Count Harrach, noting the event in his diary, did not single out the tragic fates of

[6] Cf. E. K. Chambers, *William Shakespeare* (Oxford, 1930), II, 343; G. E. Bentley, *The Jacobean and Caroline Stage*, II (Oxford, 1941), 391, 451.

the star-crossed lovers but, surprisingly enough, the pranks of the clown Pickelhäring, who "was very good and funny." [7] From this striking remark, as well as from the texts of the plays that have come down to us from that period, two conclusions may be drawn. First, that even Shakespeare's dramas, which we have come to venerate with an almost supernatural awe and sometimes a good deal of Bardolatry, were considered, in the old days, simply as a source of amusement and delight. Secondly, that the versions of the plays, as they were produced by strolling actors either in English, or more often in German, were a very far cry from the original texts printed in the First Folio or the good Quartos. [8]

The first versions of Shakespeare in the Czech language appeared toward the end of the eighteenth century. At that period of the American and French revolutions, the Czechs and Slovaks were also in process of a national awakening and they turned to Shakespeare as one of their mightiest allies. The beginnings, however, were very incon-

[7] Ernst Harrach's Family Archives are preserved in Vienna; a copy is kept in Prague, State Central Archives, collection of copies (Vienna 25.6. 1658). When checking the data about English and German strolling players, I was helped by Mr. Josef Petráň of the Department of Czechoslovak History and Archives Studies of Charles University, Prague.

[8] Some of the German texts were edited by A. Cohn in *Shakespeare in Germany* (London, 1865): *Tragedy of Titus Andronicus, Tragedy of Fratricide Punished or Prince Hamlet of Denmark, Tragedy of Romeo and Juliet.* Also by J. Meissner, *Die englischen Comoedianten zur Zeit Shakespeares in Oesterreich* (Vienna, 1884): *Comoedia Genandt Dass Wohl Gesprochene Uhrtheil Eynes Weiblichen Studenten oder der Jud von Venedig.* See also O. Tauber, *Geschichte des Prager Theaters,* I (Prague, 1883); F. Menčík, *Příspěvky k dějinám českého divadla,* Rozpravy České akademie, tř. III, roč. IV, č. 1 (Prague, 1895).

spicuous. In 1782 there appeared in South Bohemia two curious chapbooks bearing the titles *The Merchant of Venice, or Love and Friendship (Kupec z Wenedyku, nebo Láska a Přátelstvo)* and *Macbeth, Leader of the Scotch Army (Makbet Wůdce Ssottského Wogska).*[9] In their subtitles and prefaces the little volumes stated that they were translations from German "comedies" and were prepared for the lovers of the Czech language who could not see the plays in the big towns and cities. In other words, these were two popular winter's tales giving a reasonably faithful paraphrase in prose of the actions and characters of Shakespeare's plays. Disarmingly naïve as both the anonymous narratives are, they may claim priority, as far as I know, among the first modern tales from Shakespeare, preceding by a quarter of a century the well-known *Tales* of Charles and Mary Lamb. Even the infinite riches of the Folger Library do not offer an earlier specimen of a modern Shakespearean tale than *The History of King Lear and His Three Daughters . . . Written for the Amusement and Instruction of Youth* and published in London in 1794.[10]

The first real play by Shakespeare in Czech was published in 1786. It was a prose version of *Macbeth* by K. H. Thám, the leading spirit of a whole group of young patriots who founded in Prague a theater known popularly as the "Booth" (because it was built of wood, like Shakespeare's Globe). In succeeding years three other Czech translations of Shakespeare's tragedies were produced in

---

[9] A modern reprint of the two tales from Shakespeare was edited by V. Müller in one mimeographed volume (Prague, 1954).

[10] I am indebted to Miss Dorothy Mason for kindly pointing out this book to me among the holdings of the Folger Shakespeare Library.

Prague: *King Lear, Hamlet,* and *Romeo and Juliet* (the last two translations have been lost). They were all based on German theatrical adaptations and provided with happy endings or other drastic changes according to the taste of the "age of reason." No wonder they made a modern Czech scholar and translator sigh in despair that "Shakespeare came to Bohemia mangled beyond recognition." [11] Nevertheless, these clumsy first steps were improved by further attempts in the first half of the nineteenth century both in Bohemia and in Slovakia. The most successful were those by J. K. Tyl (1808–1856), our popular playwright, story writer, and actor, who made lively dramatic versions of *King Lear* (produced 1835), scenes from *1 Henry IV* (produced 1836) and from *Macbeth* and *Romeo and Juliet* (the last two have not been recovered).[12] The first memorable contribution of Czech Shakespearean criticism appeared in 1847, when the utopian socialist F. M. Klácel combined a keen sense of Hegelian dialectics and of the social implications of art in his brief but penetrating observations on the dramas of Shakespeare, Goethe, and Schiller.[13]

[11] O. Fischer, "Makbeth v Čechách," in W. Shakespeare, *Makbeth* (Prague, 1937), p. 101.

[12] The manuscript of Tyl's translation of *King Lear* was discovered only recently in northeast Bohemia. It was analyzed by O. Vočadlo in the article "J. K. Tyl a Shakespeare," *Listy z dějin českého divadla I* (Prague, 1954), pp. 9–26. See also by the same author "Český Shakespeare" (as described in footnote 5), pp. 24–31. Tyl's scenes from *1 Henry IV* were edited by Jar. Procházka: *Tylův Shakespeare v Kajetánském divadle* (Prague, 1964).

[13] F. M. Klácel, "Shakespeare. Goethe. Schiller," *Časopis Českého museum* XXI (1847), 250–269. In 1869 Klácel left Bohemia for the United States, where he worked, mostly as editor and educator, in Iowa City, Milwaukee, Racine, Chicago, Cooperstown, Kossuthtown, Kewaunee; he died at Belle Plaine in 1882.

Shakespeare in Czechoslovakia

On the whole, it is difficult to exaggerate the importance of Shakespeare for the Czech and Slovak literary revival. Our first Shakespearean translators and actors attempted, with an almost foolhardy audacity, to render Shakespeare's poem-plays into Czech and so prove to themselves and to the whole world that our idiom was able to express the highest achievements of world culture. Shakespeare helped our language, which by the end of the eighteenth century survived only among peasants, artisans, and servants, to become again the speech of kings and great heroes. And, conversely, his great heroes were adopting the indelible speech of our people. Thus Shakespeare's work was turning into one of the cornerstones of our reviving national culture.

All these early endeavors prepared the ground for the complete metrical translation of Shakespeare's plays into Czech. It appeared in separate volumes around the year 1864 as a collective work of five translators (J. Malý, F. Doucha, J. R. Čejka, J. J. Kolár, and L. J. Čelakovský).[14] Their "Museum Edition" was a permanent tribute to the tercentenary of Shakespeare's birth, which was celebrated as "the greatest festival of our new art," enlisting the participation not only of translators, actors, and critics but also of musical composers (B. Smetana, V. Blodek), painters (K. Purkyně), sculptors (J. Čapek, Sr.), etc. When we read that the festivities reached their culmination in a pageant of 230 leading citizens of Prague, who marched in Shakespearean costumes and paid homage to

[14] The whole edition was launched in 1855 with the translation of *Richard III* and could be closed, because of financial and other difficulties, only in 1872 by *Pericles*. In the following year it was accompanied by the first Czech full-length monograph on Shakespeare by one of the translators, J. Malý, *Shakespear a jeho tvorba* (Shakespeare and His Work).

the Bard "in front of his colossal bust," it may sound as pompous to us today as the accounts of Garrick's Jubilee at Stratford-on-Avon in 1769. There can be little doubt, however, that the participants enjoyed themselves and, moreover, experienced a shock of recognition for the play-wright who was helping them to feel equal and inde-pendent among other cultural nations of the world.

By this time Czech Shakespearean criticism also reached its first maturity in the reviews and essays of our two major writers and poets, V. Hálek and J. Neruda. The latter should be remembered for his clear-sighted interpretation of Shylock, whom he saw neither as a mere clown (as some German critics did), nor as a romantically tragic avenger of Jewry, but as a true-to-life, realistic character of a Jewish merchant, reflecting all the contradictory aspects of his his-torical and social plight.[15]

The poetic qualities of Shakespeare's art were fully ap-preciated and creatively expressed around the turn of the nineteenth century by two national poets, J. V. Sládek (who translated thirty-three of the plays into Czech) and P. O. Hviezdoslav (who dressed *Hamlet* and *A Midsum-mer Night's Dream* in Slovak costumes, as he himself put it). Sládek in particular deserves recognition. He mastered the English language during his two-year stay in the United States (1868–1870), crossing it from Chicago to the Gulf of Mexico, earning money in all sorts of jobs, writing both poems and prose, and translating Longfel-low's *The Song of Hiawatha*. The last twenty-five years of his life he devoted primarily to Shakespeare, and undoubt-

[15] Jan Neruda, "Shylok clown či Jidáš Machabejský?" *Literární listy,* June 24, 1865. Modern reprint by Z. Stříbrný in the Czech edition of *The Merchant of Venice* (Prague, 1955), pp. 186–189.

edly his painstakingly accurate yet inspired translations contributed to a new Shakespearean revival in the National Theater in Prague.

Here the tercentenary celebrations of Shakespeare's death in 1916 became once more a rallying point for Czech culture, when producer J. Kvapil, undaunted by the discouragement of the Hapsburg authorities, carried through an impressive Shakespearean cycle of fifteen plays. The stage was dominated by the great actor E. Vojan, who took eight roles. His biblically majestic Shylock, his movingly foolish, fond old man Lear, his Othello, equally passionate and noble in both love and suffering, his usurper Macbeth, torn between ambition and horror, his unpathetic Hamlet, highly sensitive to all the whips and scorns of time and the oppressor's wrong, or his Richard III, a fascinating type of a tyrant on the throne, all of them have become legends in the minds and memories of the oldest living generation. The cycle was opened by F. X. Šalda, professor of western literatures at the Charles University, who followed the old tradition in addressing another bust of Shakespeare with "a critical apostrophe," invoking Shakespeare's freedom-loving and freedom-inspiring genius. The whole cycle developed into an outspoken cultural demonstration, indicating that, after three hundred years of subjection, our people were ready to take not only their culture but also their government into their own hands.

Since 1918, in the newly created Czechoslovak republic, the Shakespearean revival continued unhampered for twenty years, both in the Czech lands and in Slovakia, where the first professional theaters were founded. Producer Kvapil went on attracting Prague audiences with original and mature stagings of many more plays of the

Shakespeare canon, some of them less known and less hack-
neyed. His *Troilus and Cressida* (1921), in a baroque setting, was the first satisfactory production of this difficult
problem play in the Czech theater, because it managed to
blend all the divergent elements of tragedy, grotesque,
parody, and satire into a multiple artistic unity. In his
Winter's Tale he gave a special stress to the Bohemian
scenes, making them picturesque with features of Prague
Gothic architecture, Czech landscape, and Slavic folklore
costumes, songs, and dances.

Gradually there developed quite a fruitful encounter
between the older methods of Shakespearean interpretation and the new translators (B. Štěpánek, later E. A.
Saudek) and producers (K. H. Hilar, later J. Frejka, E. F.
Burian), who were responding to the development of
modern Czech poetic language as well as modern European staging. Especially the volcanic and rather erratic
personality of K. H. Hilar was responsible for some daring
ventures which pointed the way to future experiment.
Among them, the performances of *Romeo and Juliet*
(1924) and *Hamlet* (1926) were particularly successful in
communicating the disillusions, frustrations, and passionate longings of the postwar lost generation. Even outside
Prague some memorable avant-gardist performances were
put on in the thirties (in particular by O. Stibor in
Olomouc, V. Šulc in Bratislava, and the actor-producer J.
Skřivan in Brno). A whole pleiad of young Shakespearean actors appeared. If I were to choose only one of them
by way of example, I would name Z. Štěpánek for his ver-
satility and unflagging creative energy during the period
between the two world wars and on to the present day. His
Shakespearean roles are difficult to count, and we find

among them such very different characters as Bassanio, Polixenes, Petruchio, Touchstone, Antony, Brutus, Richard III, Caliban, Macbeth, Othello, Shylock, and Lear.

The Munich Pact of 1938 and the Nazi occupation of the Czech lands in the following year brought a violent end to these promising openings. Some of the most lively producers and actors perished in the concentration camps, others survived in conditions which by no means allowed them a free expression of their talents. An encouraging event of this depressing period was the publication of Professor F. Chudoba's *Book about Shakespeare.*[16] Its two volumes, published in the years 1941–1943, summed up the lifelong devotion of the Moravian scholar to Shakespeare and opened a treasure house of humanity in the midst of inhumanity.

After the liberation in 1945, Shakespearean activities were resumed with added zest. They have had a firm basis in the rapid expansion of both professional and amateur theaters as well as in the foundation of theater arts schools with university status. The number of professional theaters has increased three times, and although some of the new companies have had to fight hard for their existence, with competition from films and television, all of Czechoslovakia's sixty or so professional theaters have found Shakespeare their best mainstay.

The oppressive experience of Nazi occupation haunted some Shakespearean productions in the first years after the war, in particular those of *Macbeth* in Prague (Municipal Theater, 1946), Olomouc (1946–1947) and Pilsen (1948–1949). The avant-garde Prague producer E. F. Burian

[16] František Chudoba, *Kniha o Shakespearovi,* I (Prague, 1941), 815; II, in 12 instalments (Prague, 1942–1943), 854 + 20 plates.

staged, after five years of Nazi internment, his version of
Romeo and Juliet, in which Romeo's ill-fated love was re-
fashioned into "a dream of a concentration camp prisoner." At the same time, Shakespeare's comedies were becoming ever more popular and they started a tour of the
whole country, finding their way even to audiences who
had never before come to know and appreciate the best
achievements of world culture. Perhaps the most conspicuous success was scored by the buoyant farce of *The Merry
Wives of Windsor* and *The Taming of the Shrew.* Later
on, the much more refined comedy of *Twelfth Night* was
winning ground.

Although it is difficult to evaluate precisely and compre-
hensively all the successes and failures of this impetuous
development, it is safe to say that in Czechoslovakia Shakespeare is becoming as much a popular playwright as he was
in his own day. In this way he is helping our present-day
culture to bridge the fatal gap which has so often developed, in the modern age, between the arts and the people.

The spectacular success of the comedies was probably
due, to some extent at least, to the fact that their Renaissance vigor matched so well with the spirit of optimism
prevailing in our society during that turbulent period of
national liberation and social upheaval. Even the rather
wistful final song of Feste in *Twelfth Night* had a confi-
dent ring for our translators, producers, actors, and audiences:

> A great while ago the world began,
> With hey, ho, the wind and the rain.

However, in the harsher times of the cold war period
and the consequent division of the world, when the con-

stant danger of a new war was combined with a growing recognition of political errors in the recent past, Hamlet's outcry, "The time is out of joint," assumed a profoundly dramatic meaning. To be sure, Shakespeare's comedies continue to be popular. But fresh excitement and discussion center around new productions of the tragedies. Two of them, both playing at the National Theater in Prague, have evoked much comment, and I propose to dwell on them in more detail.

Since 1959 a thought-provoking *Hamlet,* directed by J. Pleskot, has continued to captivate the imagination of our public. The striking effect of the production begins with J. Svoboda's stage set based on the simple Elizabethan scene, which is made dynamic by means of modern materials and machinery. We see nothing but long black vertical panels, shifting rapidly with each change of scene into different patterns and dimly reflecting lights, torches, swords, cups, costumes, and bodies in motion. The ghost of Hamlet's father appears only as a whirl of spotlights abruptly transfixed. Light is altogether an important dramatic factor. The performance develops not as a series of famous monologues but as a thrilling revenge drama of high internal and external tension. This is achieved at some cost to Shakespeare's poetry, which is stripped not only of all romantic exuberance but sometimes even of its genuine Renaissance imagery. As if a straight question were asked by the whole play: "Are you able to face Hamlet's cruel truth, even when speaking daggers, or will you run away from it in guilty confusion and cowardice like King Claudius?" Hamlet himself is a young man of noble mind and courage. He delays his revenge mainly because he wants to penetrate to the very roots of evil, being aware of the responsibility and

complexity of all his actions. His lines are pronounced
without the slightest pose or histrionics—only his taut face
reveals the depth of his suffering and his passionate search
for justice. His restraint, bursting into coarseness and ob-
scenity rather than bombastic declamations, evokes ready
response, especially among the young generation who ac-
claim him as their hero.

The anger, even the arrogance, of youth, but also its
pure passion and self-sacrifice, find full expression in the
latest production of *Romeo and Juliet*, which opened at
the National Theater during the 1963–1964 season under
the direction of O. Krejča. Admittedly, it has been influenced by Franco Zeffirelli's spectacular performance,
brought to Prague by the Old Vic Company in 1962, and
even by the American musical *West Side Story*. Nevertheless, it remains essentially an original modern Czech interpretation of the tragedy, somewhat one-sided and briskly
updated but certainly engrossing. Again, a strong impression is made by Svoboda's scenery, requiring almost acro-
batic skills of the actors. Still more striking is the translator's and the producer's reading of the text. Romeo's
words at Juliet's tomb are lifted from their particular
setting and context and raised to the quality of a dramatic
motto of general significance:

> The time and my intents are savage-wild,
> More fierce and more inexorable far
> Than empty tigers or the roaring sea.[17]

Instead of the static beauty of traditional performances,
we are plunged into a world of dynamic clash and conflict;
instead of stylized speeches, faces, and costumes, we are
confronted with disheveled, homely, rough words and

[17] *Romeo and Juliet*, V.iii.37–39.

characters. Above all, an impatient and impassioned protest is voiced against the pettiness, quarrelsomeness, and coldhearted cruelty of the old generation who have made the world a shambles. By contrast, human tolerance and love are stressed as the highest values.

The new productions of *Hamlet* and *Romeo and Juliet* have provoked divergent reactions. Yet when all the sound and fury of discussion is spent, three indisputable facts remain. Firstly, despite their unconventionality, both productions are essentially true to Shakespeare's originals—much more so, in fact, than some pre- and post-war adaptations of the two plays in our avant-garde theaters. Secondly, the new interpretations are in accord with the traditional Czech approach to Shakespeare, which has always tended to combine aesthetic enjoyment with moral and political issues of the times. Finally, it seems that the modern productions of *Hamlet* and *Romeo and Juliet* have again established the Czech National Theater as the leading center of our Shakespearean interpretation. For a truly national theater should not only preserve the best values of the past but also interpret them in such a way that they indicate new developments in human sensibility, thinking, and action—exactly as Shakespeare's theater did in his own time.

It would probably be proper to close my talk by giving you a full survey of this year's quatercentenary celebrations of Shakespeare's birth in my country. I suspect, however, that we all are, by this time of year, somewhat "tired with all these," to use a Shakespearean phrase. Therefore, allow me to say quite briefly that, of course, there have been many Shakespearean performances and whole drama festivals, including the visit of the Royal Shakespeare

Company from Stratford-on-Avon, who came to Prague with *King Lear* and *The Comedy of Errors* as the much more elegant and sophisticated successors of the old English strolling comedians of Shakespeare's own age. There have been many new publications by and about Shakespeare, the most significant among them being Shakespeare's complete works in the classical translation of J. V. Sládek and his collaborators, re-edited with a rich scholarly commentary by Professor O. Vočadlo.[18] There has been another direct address to Shakespeare, this time in the form of an imaginary letter sent to his Stratford home by our best comic actor Jan Werich, who explains to the Bard why he could not resist the temptation of translating and adapting the two parts of *Henry IV* into a *Merry Play about the Sorrows of Aging of Sir John Falstaff*.[19] There have been more tales from Shakespeare for Czech children by E. Vrchlická, actress of the Prague National Theater.[20] There have been many lectures on Shakespeare and whole cycles of lectures and several conferences at which translators, scholars, critics, producers, and actors were cudgeling their brains, or cudgeling each other, with the evergreen problems of how to interpret Shakespeare. There have been Shakespearean exhibitions, concerts, films, and radio and TV programs. There has been again a marked growth of Shakespearean inspiration in Czech and Slovak music, painting, sculpture, drama, fiction, and po-

[18] W. Shakespeare, *Komedie I–II* (Prague, 1959); *Tragédie I–II* (Prague, 1962); *Historie I, Historie II–Básně* (Prague, 1964).

[19] Werich's letter and the text of his adaptation were published in the Shakespearean issue of the monthly *Divadlo* ("The Theater"), June, 1964, pp. 91–119.

[20] Eva Vrchlická, *Zoříšku královny Mab. Povídky ze Shakespeara* (first edition, Prague, 1946; enlarged re-edition, Prague, 1964).

etry.[21] Indeed, there is no end of Shakespeare in the Czechoslovakia of 1964.

And yet, to be quite sincere, I should add that during all these innumerable celebrations the occasions were rather rare when I could feel in real touch with Shakespeare. Certainly, we cannot avoid celebrating him with all due

[21] Since their first performances in 1946 and 1959 respectively, I. Krejčí's comic opera *Pozdvižení v Efesu* (based on *The Comedy of Errors*) and J. Hanuš' ballet *Othello* have been often on the stage; recently Zb. Vostrák has composed a vocal cycle to Shakespeare's *Sonnets;* V. Kabeláč's *Hamletovská improvizace* was played for the first time on May 26, 1964. In the same year a set of five long-playing records reproducing Shakespearean words and music was published, accompanied by the book *Shakespeare v hudbě a na našem jevišti* ("Shakespeare in Music and on Our Stage") by J. Bachtík, J. Berkovec, J. Pokorný, and L. Lajcha. Other books of the quatercentenary year include Z. Stříbrný's paperback *William Shakespeare,* a selection of Shakespearean criticism translated and edited by B. Hodek under the title *Shakespeare a moderní divadlo* ("Shakespeare and the Modern Theater"), and the Czech translation of the Shakespearean essays by the Polish critic Jan Kott. All the books were published in Prague.

Among the Czechoslovak painters who have recently contributed to Shakespearean themes special mention should be made of L. Jiřincová, J. Zrzavý, J. Šíma, K. Svolinský, M. Troup, J. Liesler, K. Hruška, Vl. Tesař. A memorial medal was created by M. Knobloch and a bas-relief by J. Kodet.

Shakespeare's influence can be marked in some of the plays of the young dramatist J. Topol, who has also translated *Romeo and Juliet* (Prague, 1964); one of the leading novelists, J. Otčenášek, has written a short novel about the love of a Jewish girl and a Czech boy during the Nazi occupation of Bohemia with the title *Romeo a Julie a tma* ("Romeo and Juliet and Darkness," first published in Prague, 1959; fifth edition 1963); a short historical novel by M. Kratochvíl, *Komediant* ("The Comedian," Prague, 1962) gives the story of a group of strolling players performing *Romeo and Juliet* during the Thirty Years' War; finally, our major poet, Vl. Holan, has published his *Noc s Hamletem* ("Night with Hamlet") toward the end of the quatercentenary.

homage once or twice in a century. However, it is good to think again of the less festive and more workaday times when he goes with us to be our guide in our need. And we can only hope that he may really become a part of the daily culture and the daily life of every man. For we shall probably all agree that now, as ever, his humanizing touch is most needed both in the West and the East.

Shakespeare's Sonnets as Literature[*]

By SERGIO BALDI

IN 1609, a well-known (but not too well-known) London publisher, Thomas Thorpe, brought forth a small quarto volume of some eighty pages, simply entitled *Shakespeare's Sonnets, Never Before Imprinted*. This small quarto contained 154 sonnets and a longer poem entitled "A Lover's Complaint." It was dedicated to a Mr. W. H., "the only begetter of these ensuing sonnets," to whom the publisher wished "all happiness, and that eternity promised by our ever-living poet." On June 19, Edward Alleyn, the actor, paid fivepence for it.

We do not know to what extent Shakespeare was concerned with the printing of his sonnets. On the other hand, we know that they had been circulated in manuscript for a time, because ten years before, in 1598, Francis

---

[*] Delivered on November 22, 1964. Mr. Baldi is a professor of English language and literature at the University of Florence.

Meres had written that Shakespeare's "sugared sonnets" could favorably compare with Ovid's poems. This does not mean at all that Shakespeare was anxious to see them in print. At the end of the sixteenth century and even afterward there were people who still considered the press too vulgar a means for the circulation of love poems; for all we know, Shakespeare might have either authorized the publication of his sonnets or been completely unaware of it. Publishers are known to have made themselves free with Shakespeare's name and work. In the same year, 1598 (or the year after), William Jaggard had published a whole anthology of lyric verse under Shakespeare's name, although only five of these poems were actually his. Shakespeare complained, but not too loudly: anyhow his complaints did not prevent this anthology from reaching a third edition.

The problem of Shakespeare's participation in the printing of the sonnets is more than a mere matter of curiosity. In fact, if we believe that Shakespeare himself had nothing to do with their publication (as he had nothing to do with Jaggard's *Passionate Pilgrim*), Thorpe's attribution, text, and order are of very little consequence and the modern editor is authorized to do all he can to give the modern reader Shakespeare's text and order as he meant them. On the other hand, if we believe that Thorpe's edition was authorized and prepared by Shakespeare himself, the modern editor may only presume to correct the clerical errors of the printer.

Both theories have been held, and much quarreling has ensued among editors. A brilliant way out has been found lately by J. Dover Wilson, who maintains that the first 126 sonnets belong to a manuscript which was, "if not Shakespeare's autograph, . . . a tolerably competent transcript of such an autograph," while the last twenty-eight sonnets are but "a miscellaneous and disorderly appendix," probably not wholly Shakespeare's. If so, Thorpe's intervention in Shakespeare's copy would not have been great—at least from the point of view of an Elizabethan publisher.

On the whole, this seems to me a very tenable proposition. The first seventeen sonnets have in common a practical aim: to persuade a young man to marry. The sonnets from the 18th to the 126th are all addressed to a beautiful young man. The remaining twenty-eight sonnets, on the contrary, have no unity, although most of them are about a dark woman neither beautiful nor faithful, yet physically attractive. According to these quite obvious features, it is customary to divide Shakespeare's sonnets into three groups: the "marriage group," that is, the first seventeen sonnets; the "Young Friend group," that is, the central 109 sonnets; the "Dark Woman group," that is, the last twenty-eight sonnets. I see no reason for major changes in this grouping, yet it must be observed that the "Young Friend group" has not the homogeneity of the "marriage group." While the latter has an indisputable consistency, both in aim and style, this cannot be said of the "Young Friend group," the sonnets of which—if taken separately—cannot all be said to be addressed to a young man. Moreover, there is an undeniable evolution in style.

Our wish to know who the Young Friend, the Dark Woman, the Rival Poet, might have been in life, is a legitimate wish but cannot be satisfied. There is a general tendency among Shakespearean scholars to assume that the famous initials, "W. H.," stand either for Henry Wriothesley, Earl of Southampton, or for William Herbert, Earl of

Pembroke. This is an everlasting quarrel, but in fact there is very little evidence to support either assumption; consequently, other Williams, and even a Hugh, have been proposed. An attempt has also been made to distribute the sonnets between the two peers—an attempt which has been too rapidly discarded, in my opinion.

I shall go a little further and say that personally I do not believe that all the first 126 sonnets were addressed to the same person. This amounts to saying that I do not believe that "Mr. W. H." was "the only begetter" of all Shakespeare's sonnets. I do not even believe that all Petrarch's sonnets were written for Laura de Sade, or that the whole of Sidney's *Astrophel and Stella* was written for Penelope Devereux. On the contrary, I do believe that Laura, Stella, and the Young Friend were like magnetic poles in the field of poetic imagination, around which several different but similar moments have gathered. But I am not going to argue this point now. Let it suffice for the moment that the sonnets of the first and second groups are about an *ideal* love for an *ideal* beautiful youth, and that Shakespeare was able to give poetical expression to this ideal love. From my point of view, it does not matter at all whether this ideal love found one or many empirical realizations—"shadows," Shakespeare would say: the several experiences—if several experiences they were—have not broken the sentimental unity of the sonnets.

I shall press this point a little further. The sex itself of the Young Friend is of no importance. This point was admirably stated by the late Professor C. S. Lewis ten years ago, when he wrote:

From [the] total plot [of Shakespeare's sonnets], however ambiguous, however particular, there emerges something not indeed common or general like the love expressed in many individual sonnets but yet, in a higher way, universal. The main contrast in the *Sonnets* is between two loves, that "of comfort" and that "of despair." The love "of despair" demands all; the love "of comfort" asks, and perhaps receives, nothing. . . . And so it comes about that, however the whole thing began—in perversion, in convention, even (who knows?) in fiction—Shakespeare . . . ends by expressing simply love, the quintessence of all loves whether erotic, parental, filial, amicable, or feudal.

Let us accept this idea of "quintessence of love." It may be of use, above all, to justify the ways of poetry to man and help us to overcome any moralistic or physiological prejudice which might hinder us from enjoying the pure poetry of the sonnets. On the other hand, we must be careful not to infer that this "quintessence of love" had no actual counterpart in life. Shakespeare's was an *ideal* love, not an *abstract* love. Hence all the human aspects of love: the exaltation of the beloved and the humiliation of the lover, the sorrows of absence and the joy of being near each other, definite and indefinite fears, reciprocal jealousy and betrayals, repentance and reconciliation. This is the story of Ovid's *Amores,* but it is also everybody's and everyday's story. I have no doubt that this is also a true story, that is, that the Young Friend, the Dark Woman, the Rival Poet, were actual people, and, too, that the greater part of the sonnets, if not all, arose from actual situations. A number of them are even letters or parts of letters. But this is just the magic of poetry: to transform a transient fact of private interest into "something rich and strange," a universal experience of universal human interest.

Nevertheless, Shakespeare did not effect this transformation independently from the literary conventions of his time. These are, as it were, Shakespeare's poetical lan-

guage. Against the well-known Crocean idea, that the poet
creates his own language, I would rather assume the more
recent concept of "reciprocal continuous influence" between the "received language" and the "message" of the
poet—a kind of "reciprocal conditioning." To illustrate a
few of the more distinctive features of this exchange will
now be my task.

The most evident feature of Shakespeare's sonnets is
that they are sonnets. I shall not go into the history of the
meter. Shakespeare did not invent the so-called "Shakespearean form" of the sonnet, which was a well-established
form when he wrote. Moreover, at the end of the sixteenth
century, although the sonnet admitted of several metrical
forms, it was almost the approved genre for love poems. In
this sense Shakespeare also merely followed the literary
convention of his times. In fact, when Shakespeare wrote
his sonnets, poets had been writing poems of that kind for
more than three hundred years, and, of all the sonnet writers, Francis Petrarch was certainly the most famous. So
famous was he, especially in the sixteenth century, that in
most literary histories of the Renaissance "Petrarchism"
has almost become synonymous with "sonnet writing."

Of course, Shakespeare's sonnets cannot be defined as
Petrarchan in any way; moreover, European Petrarchism in
the sixteenth century was quite a different thing from
Petrarch's own poetry. Yet certain features of Shakespeare's sonnets, besides their meter, can be traced back to
the Petrarchan convention, or better, to a literary convention of courtly love that even Petrarch had followed—at
least to a certain extent. This convention appears to have
arisen in Provence in the latter half of the thirteenth century. According to it, the relation between the Lover and

the Beloved is represented in feudal terms, as the relation between the Vassal and the Lord. The Lover accepts the Beloved as his *Lord* (notwithstanding her being a woman —the feudal convention is stronger than sense, at least in the beginning); and thus the Lover becomes her *vassal,* swears *loyalty* to her, pays her *homage.* On the other hand, the *Lord* (the woman in this case) must grant her *vassal* the due *reward:* if she does so, she is *bountiful* and equal to her *merit;* if she does not, she is *unkind* and will be disgraced. I said above that Petrarch himself follows this convention up to a certain point; Shakespeare does not follow it at all. Yet the general idea of expressing the relation between Lover and the Beloved in feudal terms lingered well beyond the fourteenth century, and the sonnet writers of the Renaissance preserved the use of its technical words even when their precise meaning was lost; moreover they preserved the sense of "absolute submission" and "anxious expectation" that went with them. Absolute submission and anxious expectation are to be found in Shakespeare too and will be dealt with later on. Let us notice, now, that a few relics of the feudal love language can still be found in Shakespeare's sonnets—for instance, at the beginning of Sonnet 26: "Lord of my love, to whom in vassalage / Thy merit hath my duty strongly knit." Here, notwithstanding "lord," "vassalage," "merit," and "duty," Shakespeare's language is neither feudal nor Petrarchan. In fact, at the end of the sixteenth century, the pure Petrarchan tradition was almost dead throughout Europe: in England both Spenser with his *Shepheardes Calendar* and Sidney with his *Astrophel and Stella* had already left Petrarch for Ronsard and the Pléiade poets—who styled themselves "antipétrarquistes," that is, "against Petrarch."

They had left Petrarch and the conventions and language of courtly love for the new conventions and language of Neoplatonic love lore. The Neoplatonism of the Renaissance was born in Florence in the second half of the fifteenth century; but while in Italy it *added* to the Petrarchan tradition and created a new phase *within* the movement itself, in France Neoplatonism in poetry opposed Petrarchism and started a literary quarrel. There was no quarrel in England, yet the discrepancy is still wider and more evident in English literature on account of the very poor years (poor in poetry) that separate the death of Surrey in 1547 and the publication of *The Shepheardes Calendar* in 1579.

It is then consonant with the spirit of the times that Shakespeare's sonnets are Platonic in spirit: such were, for instance, Sidney's and Daniel's before them. But in Shakespeare's case his Platonism is stressed by the Beloved being a boy, a beautiful youth whose friendship is passionately sought after. More than twenty-five years ago, in 1927, Alfred Noyes pointed out that the acme of the sonnets is to be seen in Sonnet 116, "Let me not to the marriage of true minds / Admit impediments," and aptly said that this sonnet "deals with love as an Absolute," as a Platonic absolute, we would add, having in mind the second speech of Socrates in Plato's *Phaedrus*.

We cannot say how much of Plato Shakespeare read, nor if he read it in the original Greek or in a Latin translation, nor even if he read it at all or knew of it at second hand. Ben Jonson said that Shakespeare "had small Latin and less Greek," but we should not trust a rival playwright too far. Yet it is a fact that Sonnet 144, "Two loves I have, of comfort and despair, / Which like two spirits do suggest me still: / The better angel is a man right fair, / The worser spirit a woman color'd ill," poses again Plato's distinction between a kind of love moved by sensuality (which Socrates condemned) and a kind of love which stands "with modesty upon a pedestal of chastity." Moreover, Shakespeare's attitude toward the Young Friend follows step by step the behavior of the "followers of Apollo" as represented by Socrates.

[The followers of Apollo, says he] go out and seek for their beloved a youth whose nature accords with that of the god, and when they have gained his affection, by imitating the god themselves, and by persuasion and education, they lead the beloved to the conduct and nature of the god, so far as each of them can do so; they exhibit no jealousy or meanness toward the loved one, but endeavor by every means in their power to lead him to the likeness of the god they honor.

These words may serve to explain the tutorial attitude toward the Young Friend that pervades the sonnets. The Poet wants the Friend to marry both for aesthetic and practical reasons; he is ready to forgive his sins as "petty wrongs that liberty commits," he is ready to forgive him even his betrayal of friendship in taking the Dark Woman away from him, thus exhibiting "no jealousy or meanness." The failure of the pupil is the failure of the teacher. In fact, the Young Friend is asked to "climb upon the ladder" of spiritual perfection, together with the Poet, if he wants to, with a worthier teacher if such can be found. Shakespeare is conscious of his shortcomings as well as his goodwill; remember Sonnet 85: "I think good thoughts, whilst others write good words, / And like unletter'd clerk still cry 'Amen' / To every hymn that able spirit affords / In polish'd form of well-refined pen." Only when the Young Friend seems reluctant to ascend the ladder of perfection, the Poet dares reproach him: "But why thy odor matcheth not thy show, / The soil is this, that thou dost common grow" (Sonnet 69).

According to Plato, the vision of perfect beauty and heavenly immortality is the reward of the ascent. In the *Symposium* he distinguished between two species of immortality: a kind of natural immortality, such as mortal things can acquire through reproduction; heavenly immortality, that man may acquire through moral perfection. In the sonnets of the "marriage group" Shakespeare made ample use of the idea of natural immortality, starting from the very first lines, "From fairest creatures we desire increase, / That thereby beauty's rose might never die." In the "Young Friend group," however, he seems to abandon Plato's idea of heavenly immortality for the idea of immortality through indirect fame, that is, such fame as one may acquire if one is the subject of a great poem. Such promises of indirect fame already had been made by Greek and Latin poets, but never to such an extent as they were made afterward by the poets of the Renaissance. In Sonnet 55, "Not marble nor the gilded monuments / Of princes shall outlive this powerful rhyme," Shakespeare leans heavily on Horace and Ovid, like many of his predecessors: yet it is quite clear from other sonnets that the idea of immortality had for him more than a rhetorical or philosophical interest. Although in a few cases Shakespeare boasts that he is giving immortality to the *name* of the Young Friend, he is certainly much more concerned with the immortality of the Young Friend's *beauty* than with that of his name.

The Young Friend's beauty is in fact the basic theme of the sonnets. This beauty too is framed in a Platonic picture. The Young Friend has no need of the splendid vision of Ideal Beauty, he *is* ideal beauty, from which all mortal beauties descend, and thus he is all one with Truth, for Truth and Beauty are all one for Plato. "What is your substance, whereof are you made, / That millions of strange shadows on you tend?" Shakespeare asks in Sonnet 53, and "Both truth and beauty on my love depends," he will state in Sonnet 101: one could not be more explicitly Platonic. The theme of the Young Friend's beauty, of course, is not limited to a few Platonic assertions. As the theme of Ideal Beauty originated Platonic myths and images in Plato's dialogues, so it originates Shakespearean myths and images in Shakespeare's sonnets. The "millions of strange shadows" that "tend" on the Young Friend seem to cover all aspects of reality without being able to equal him. The "forward violet" of Sonnet 99 stole its sweet smell from the Young Friend's breath, and so did all flowers steal something from him: "More flowers I noted, yet I none could see / But sweet or color had it stolen from thee"; the summer's day cannot sustain comparison with the Young Friend, who is "more lovely and more temperate" (Sonnet 18); nor can Adonis, nor Helen, nor "the fairest wights" of antiquity: "So all their praises are but prophecies / Of this our time, all you prefiguring" (Sonnet 106). Vice itself becomes beautiful if embodied in the Young Friend, "Where beauty's veil doth cover every blot" (Sonnet 95); even poetical imagination becomes impotent before him: the Poet "can afford / No praise to thee but what in thee doth live" (Sonnet 79).

The critic who will notice that the beauty of the Young Friend is poetically depicted through images that logically state poetry's impossibility of doing so, will also remember

that Shakespeare himself was aware of that poetical trick—
at least when he wrote, in Sonnet 81, "Your monument
shall be my gentle verse, / Which eyes not yet created shall
o'erread; / And tongues to be your being shall rehearse, /
When all the breathers of this world are dead."

Yet, the assumption of the Young Friend's beauty to
Platonic Ideal Beauty expresses but one moment of Shakespeare's feelings toward it, the moment of exaltation. The
counterpart, the opposite point of a sort of pendular
movement, is the moment of dejection, when mortality of
beauty seems to have the upper hand. Here is the beginning of Sonnet 65: "Since brass, nor stone, nor earth, nor
boundless sea, / But sad mortality o'ersways their power, /
How with this rage shall beauty hold a plea / Whose action is no stronger than a flower?" The two moments
coexist in Shakespeare's poetry, but it seems to me that the
"moment of mortality" is predominant. It begins rather
early. Sonnet 2, "When forty winters shall besiege thy
brow," is an invitation to marry only in its practical aim;
in fact it is a meditation on the decay of beauty, ending in
a shudder, "This were to be new made when thou art
old, / And see thy blood warm when thou feel'st it cold."

This sense of death creeps into almost all sonnets in
praise of the Young Friend's beauty. It may take the shape
of a literary convention, as in Sonnet 18, where the ending,
"But thy eternal summer shall not fade," etc., has a psychological justification at least in its being a literary screen
behind which the Poet is hiding his fears. It may creep into
an image of perfect grace, such as the image of "beauty's
rose" of Sonnet 1, which comes again in Sonnet 5 as "flowers distill'd" and "A liquid prisoner pent in walls of glass."

The image of the rose will find its culmination and death in Sonnet 54, "Sweet roses do not so; / Of their sweet deaths are sweetest odors made." This sense of death may also become a prayer, as in Sonnet 19, "Devouring Time, blunt thou the lion's paws," which ends—one must remember—with a promise of immortality.

Shakespeare's poetry is at its best, of course, when he is conscious of these incertitudes and forebodings. Thus, in the third quatrain of Sonnet 12, we read: "Then of thy beauty do I question make, / That thou among the wastes of time must go, / Since sweets and beauties do themselves forsake / And die as fast as they see others grow." In the final lines of Sonnet 64 this sense of transiency, of "fear to lose," is stressed: "Ruin hath taught me thus to ruminate, / That Time will come and take my love away. / This thought is as a death, which cannot choose / But weep to have that which it fears to lose." This verbal image, "fear to lose," is a recurrent image in the sonnets; but the "Young Friend group" closes with a certitude of loss: "Yet fear her, O thou minion of her pleasure! / She may detain, but not still keep, her treasure: / Her audit, though delay'd, answer'd must be / And her quietus is to render thee" (Sonnet 126).

The opening sonnet of the "Young Friend group," "Shall I compare thee to a summer's day," and the concluding one, "O thou, my lovely boy," which I have just quoted, may be contrasted and taken to represent *ideally* the Renaissance and the mannerist moments in Shakespeare's sonnets. As a whole, Shakespeare's sonnets may be taken to represent an instance of the well-known shift "from Elizabethan to Jacobean." The theme of beauty, which I have just analyzed, is the clearest instance of it; a similar shift can be found in the treatment of their second major theme, the theme of "absolute devotion."

The Young Friend's behavior toward the Poet might have given several reasons for complaint. He had an affair with the Dark Woman, that is, with the Poet's lover; for a time he seemed to prefer a Rival Poet to the Poet himself. In neither case did Shakespeare try either to compete or to break the friendship; on the contrary, he accepted his trials with deep humility, acknowledging the right of the Young Friend to dispose of both the Poet and the Poet's property at his will. The humility Shakespeare shows before the Rival Poet may have an ironical ring; and it probably has —though Shakespeare never thought himself so great a poet as we know he is. But Shakespeare's reactions to the Young Friend's affair with the Dark Woman—which shocked Victorian readers—are worth exploring.

The author of *Willoughby His Avisa*, a *roman à clef* published in 1594, was either misinformed, or deliberately gross, when he wrote that W. S. acted as a procurer for his friend H. W., for "he determined to see whether it would sort to a happier end for this new actor than it did with the old player" (p. 116). On the contrary, the Poet's reaction, as it appears in the sonnets, is perfectly consonant with that of the Platonic "followers of Apollo": he shows no jealousy and above all tries "to bring sense" into the "sensual fault" of the Young Friend (Sonnet 35), while making serious or jocular comments on the "identity" of the Poet and the Young Friend (Sonnets 42 and 135). Yet I do not mean to say that Shakespeare's reaction was derived from his reading of Plato, rather that his impulse toward absolute devotion was *confirmed* and *strengthened* by his reading of Plato. In fact, there is more than a bookish feeling in his sense of "absolute devotion" to a being of perfect beauty: there is a sense of "inner unworthiness" which goes much deeper into Shakespeare's soul and poetry than any literary convention either feudal or Platonic. This sense of inner unworthiness begins with Sonnet 29, "When, in disgrace with Fortune and men's eyes, / I all alone beweep my outcast state," seems to take body in a kind of "bewailed guilt" in Sonnet 36 and to indulge in self-abjection in Sonnet 57; then it soars over death in Sonnet 71, "No longer mourn for me when I am dead / Than you shall hear the surly sullen bell."

Biography has been inextricably linked with the sonnets. Thus, several causes have been pointed to for this "bewailed guilt," this sense of inner unworthiness: namely the old age of the poet, his profession of actor, actual lameness, homosexuality, and so on. Yet one cannot be too careful in avoiding a too literal interpretation of the sonnets. Insofar as poetry is concerned, I think that the best comment on the "bewailed guilt" of the sonnets is to be found in Hamlet's words to Ophelia, when in Act III he says that he is "indifferent honest," yet "with more offenses at [his] beck than [he has] thoughts to put them in, imagination to give them shape, or time to act them in." The point is that an *indifferent honest man* can have more sin at his beck than imagination to put them in, and such sins as to wish "[his] mother had never borne [him]." In much less poetical words, this means that a "sense of guilt" is much more important than "actual guilt"—and such seems to me to be the case of the sonnets. An innate sense of unworthiness seems to have given rise to Shakespeare's sense of absolute devotion to the Young Friend, or, better, to ideal beauty as embodied in the Young Friend.

A few actual images, such as "Lord of my love" (Sonnet 26), or "Being your slave" and "being your vassal" (Sonnets 37 and 38), vaguely link this theme of inner unworthiness before ideal beauty with the medieval tradition of courtly love; but it soon develops into a complacent enjoyment of this state of inferiority, a state wherein the Poet seems to be predestined for total annihilation into the supreme perfection of the Young Friend. "Let not my love be call'd idolatry," he wrote in Sonnet 105, yet, and in spite of that, he also wrote, in Sonnet 58, "That god . . . that made me first your slave," and in Sonnet 40, he had said that he was more than content to be robbed of "all [his] poverty" by such a "gentle thief." Moreover, the Poet will never say anything against the Young Friend, on the contrary he will fight on the Young Friend's side against himself (Sonnet 88); he even feels a sort of moral responsibility toward him: in Sonnet 61 he asks, "Is it thy spirit that thou send'st from thee / So far from home into my deeds to pry, / To find out shames and idle hours in me?" The love he feels for the Young Friend is an all-exacting love, and so he feels the necessity of sacrificing unto him: "Thy bosom is endeared with all hearts, / Which I by lacking have supposed dead" (Sonnet 31), and then in Sonnet 40, "Take all my loves, my love, yea, take them all; / What hast thou then more than thou hadst before?"

This almost mystical sense of unworthiness materializes into pictorial images of "cold and bareness." In Sonnet 12 ("marriage group") the "lofty trees . . . barren of leaves" induce the Poet to "question make" of the Young

Friend's beauty; later on similar images will be suggested by the "question" itself. In Sonnet 97: "How like a winter hath my absence been / . . . / What old December's bareness everywhere!" then again, in the justly famous Sonnet 73, where the theme of personal unworthiness and its images of old age and winter bareness are fused to a perfection: "That time of year thou mayst in me behold / When yellow leaves, or none, or few, do hang / Upon those boughs which shake against the cold, / Bare ruin'd choirs where late the sweet birds sang."

This theme of the unworthiness of the Poet before ideal beauty tends to move forward toward the total unworthiness of the world itself. The "vileness" of the world as a whole is certainly more widely and deeply dealt with in Shakespeare's major tragedies than in the sonnets, and in *Hamlet* more than in any other tragedy. Yet, even the reader of the sonnets may gather a few glimpses of it. There are other parallels between the sonnets and the undeserved brutalities which Hamlet bestows upon Ophelia. "God hath given you one face, and you make yourselves another," says Hamlet; and in the sonnets "a painted face" is the symbol of human wickedness. "Get thee to a nunnery! Why wouldst thou be a breeder of sinners?" says Hamlet again; and in the later sonnets the Poet seems to have lost his former faith in marriage and human reproduction. This world is a "vile" world, and the Poet is sorry and worried that the Young Friend has to live in it: "Ah, wherefore with infection should he live / And with his presence grace impiety, / That sin by him advantage should achieve / And lace itself with his society?" (Sonnet 67). With the extension to the world as a whole of the original sense of personal unworthiness, we are now a very long way off from that sense of poise and balance which is considered to be the essential feature of the Renaissance. Once again we have reached the threshold of the manneristic age.

"Nature," said Sir Philip Sidney, "never set forth the earth in so rich tapestry as divers poets have done, . . . her world is brazen, the poets only deliver a golden." This goldening of the brazen world of Nature is the work of the images, which constitute the very essence of poetry, its peculiar form and language. In the sonnets most of Shakespeare's imagery is "derived from nature," or, better, from floral nature, such as was the imagery of most poets of classical antiquity and the Renaissance. Thus, the ideal beauty of the Young Friend becomes "beauty's rose" at the very beginning, and the Young Friend himself is said to be the "only herald to the gaudy spring" (Sonnet 1). Accordingly, "a summer's day" (Sonnet 18) will be the proper image of the Friend's beauty, and later on all flowers will be chided for stealing either color or odor from him.

If the image of the splendor of beauty is summer, winter will be the obvious image of its decay. Thus, "beauty's rose" will become a "tatter'd weed" (Sonnet 2) in the Friend's old age, when he sees "Beauty o'ersnow'd and bareness everywhere" (Sonnet 5). A winter image is the image both of absence from the Friend and of old age: "old December's bareness everywhere" in Sonnet 97, and "boughs which shake against the cold" in Sonnet 73.

In *The Shepheardes Calendar* Spenser could be content with this natural imagery; Shakespeare could not do so in his sonnets. So even Sonnet 1 is the starting point of entirely different sets of images, which intermingle with the principal set of natural images. Images derived from usury and its legal and commercial terms are the most frequent among non-natural images, and we can find them from the second quatrain of Sonnet 1. The images of the first quatrain are floral, but those of the second belong to the usury set. In this second quatrain the Young Friend is accused of egotism because "[he makes] a famine where abundance lies," an image derived from Ovid (*Metamorphoses,* bk. iii); but the Ovidian image develops within a linguistically mercantile context: the Young Friend is said to be "contracted to [his] own bright eyes," and, in Sonnet 4, is called a "profitless usurer." As we go on, we find the number of such images increasing. "Beauty's rose" becomes "beauty's legacy," and the Young Friend is requested to leave an "acceptable audit" (Sonnet 4) for "beauty's treasure," the use of which "is not forbidden usury" (Sonnet 6). Notice that even in floral Sonnet 18, "summer's lease hath all too short a date," and that in Sonnet 13 the Young Friend "hold[s] in lease" his beauty. Sonnet 87 has no other imagery, and there we find terms such as "estimate," "charter," "bonds . . . determinate," "granting" and "misprision." Finally, let us remember that the concluding lines of the "Young Friend group" itself are built with images of this sort: "Her audit, though delay'd, answer'd must be, / And her quietus is to render thee" (Sonnet 126).

The "usury set" is the second largest set of images in the sonnets. We have other much smaller groups which are interesting either for their mere presence or for their particular development. One would probably expect the group related to sciences, especially to astronomy and navigation, to have at least a certain consistency, as Shakespeare lived in the so-called Age of Discovery; but such is the case for

Donne's, not for Shakespeare's sonnets. The "astronomy" which the Poet claims to have in Sonnet 14 is just medieval "astrology"; and only a slightly better case could be made for "eclipses" and "ocean." In Sonnet 60 "Crooked eclipses 'gainst his glory fight," and in Sonnet 107 "The mortal moon hath her eclipse endur'd," while the ocean appears three times in the sonnets (Sonnets 56, 64, 80), but nowhere very impressively. Other smaller groups, such as the graceful "distillation set," to which I have already referred, and the "clock and dial set," are interesting instances of the emblematic trend in the imagery of the sonnets in addition to the fundamental "beauty's rose"; other even smaller sets will show the presence of baroque corporeity. This is the case of the images related to food and eating. Many of them may be considered just as variations on the classical theme of *tempus edax* (the "devouring Time" of Sonnet 19), but not all of them. Not, for instance, the central image of Sonnet 118, "Even so, being full of your ne'er-cloying sweetness, / To bitter sauces did I frame my feeding"—an image absolutely baroque and almost repugnant to the modern ear.

This continuous interplay of Renaissance with manneristic trends is one of the outstanding features of the English Renaissance. To have found it in Shakespeare's sonnets should then be no surprise—but this is not the obvious conclusion which I meant to reach. Actually, I meant to reach no conclusion at all, but rather to show how these literary trends, the Platonic, the manneristic, and even the baroque, worked together to give their actual form to Shakespeare's sonnets. In other words, I have tried to describe the sonnets in terms of literary conventions, just to show that even Shakespeare, the poet of all ages, was also, and above all, a poet of his own age.

All men are alike basically. It is our common humanity that enables us to read and enjoy and understand both Homer and Vergil, both Dante and Shakespeare. Yet the historical environment changes. It is the historical environment that conditions the actual form of the poem, and sometimes even the subtler shades in the quality of the poetry.

Platonism did certainly shape that admiration for beauty which was naturally present in Shakespeare; it helped him to set his natural aspiration toward beauty into an accepted world image; it helped him to make his love spiritual, the center of a moral world of beauty. But, alas, the brazen world of Nature is certainly harder and sharper than the golden world of Poetry! At the very end of the sixteenth century the provisional harmony between poetical illusion and real life was breaking again, and the poets themselves began to "question make," not only of beauty but of the whole structure of the world itself, and felt themselves hovering between a "vile world" and the "vilest worms" among which they would have to dwell sooner or later.

The Renaissance accepted certitude of death stoically, satisfied with the sense of having lived rightly; the manneristic age, on the contrary, indulged in the thought of death, in the contemplation of physical decay. Shakespeare's sonnets share this indulgence in the contemplation of Death, this sense of the unworthiness of man and the world before the vision of Ideal Beauty.

In those years, poets were also feeling the impact of a

new world that could not be represented through the old imagery of the classical world: hence Shakespeare's assumption of the language of usury, of physics, of everyday life into the language of his poetry. Those were also the years when man was discovering subtler relations between spirit and matter and could be content no longer with the sharp, neat cut that had been enough for the medieval man: hence the emblematic quality of his images and their plastic and pictorial values.

Thus Shakespeare's natural "quintessential" love for beauty took "a local habitation and a name." A local habitation: Renaissance England. A name: not Mr. W. H.— William Shakespeare.

Sidney Lanier:

Amateur Shakespearean*

By FREDERICK HARD

IN selecting the title "Sidney Lanier: Amateur Shakespearean," I have used the word *amateur* in its literal
rather than in its pejorative sense. Lanier was a lover of
Shakespeare and a dedicated reader of the poet and of the
period in which he lived and worked; and his enthusiasm,
which had its roots in his father's library and continued to
grow and flower throughout his brief and difficult life, was
that of a devoted connoisseur, rather than that of a trained
and disciplined scholar.

Although as a boy he exhibited an extraordinary talent
in the field of science, and wished, in his youth, to become
a teacher of physics and mathematics, his two great spiritual and intellectual loves were literature and music. And
while his more serious loyalties sometimes shifted from one

* Delivered on December 13, 1964. Mr. Hard is president-emeritus
of Scripps College.

to the other, he was truly devoted to both, and spent much of his time, thought, and energy, under difficult circumstances, in earnest efforts to achieve professional competence in each of these fields and to promote a wider understanding of the relationship of each to the other.

If Lanier's scholarship were to be assessed in the light of our rather exacting current standards, his accomplishment would have to be regarded as meager, certainly as to its quantity, and, in some respects, as to its quality. But we may remember that when he began, late in his own life, to delve into what he called his "searchings" into the Elizabethan field, formal graduate study in English literature, which began in the United States with the founding of the Johns Hopkins University, was not yet ten years old. In those days candidates for the Ph.D. customarily went to Germany for their training, and they continued to do so for years afterwards. The development of rigorous scholarly disciplines, methods, and techniques was still in a comparatively early stage. At any rate, whatever and wherever academic opportunities might have been available, they were not available to Lanier. What he was able to do in this regard, he did for himself. He was a self-taught scholar, and what he accomplished was almost entirely on his own. The results, I believe, are not without their significant influence and value.

Lanier was also a self-taught musician. As a professional musician, however, his credentials are secure in the pages of history, and the story of his career is as remarkable as it is pathetic.

Born in the small town of Macon, Georgia, in 1842, he was brought up as a normal southern boy amid the cultural limitations of that community. Yet as a young child he was already playing the piano, flute, guitar, violin, and organ. At the age of fourteen he entered Oglethorpe College, where he organized an orchestra among his friends and was its conductor. At college he came under the influence of Professor James Woodrow (a former student of Agassiz at Harvard), who sharpened the boy's interest in science, gave him a respect for orderly studies, and inspired in him a desire to go to Germany for graduate study, whence he planned to return to Macon and to do his part in the upbuilding of the culture of his native town.

But the war put an end to these dreams, and he and his brother Clifford enlisted in the very first company that went out of Georgia to the battlefields of Virginia.

After three years of gallant service, he was captured on a blockade runner (on which he was posted as signal officer) November 2, 1864. He remained in prison at Point Lookout, Maryland, for almost all of the remainder of the war, and it is reported that he spent much of the dreary time cheering up his fellow prisoners with music from his flute, which he had smuggled into prison up his sleeve and was apparently allowed to keep.

At the close of the war he walked the painful journey through the Carolinas back home to a desolate Macon, footsore, discouraged, and seriously ill, only to find his mother dying of tuberculosis—the disease of which he himself was to become the victim.

For the next six years—indeed, for the rest of his life—he struggled against almost overwhelming handicaps, the most serious of which was illness, with its attendant poverty, which he sought to offset with a variety of occupations, including the practice of law; but in 1873 he made the momentous decision to give up these miscellaneous activities and move to Baltimore, hoping to gain a position with the Peabody Symphony Orchestra, then being organized under the conductorship of Asger Hamerik. In a letter written on November 29, Lanier tells his father, in poignant language, of the thoughts that lay behind this decision:

Why should I, nay, how *can* I, settle myself down to be a third-rate struggling lawyer for the balance of my little life as long as there is a certainty almost absolute that I can do some other things so much better. Several persons, from whose judgment there can be no appeal, have told me, for instance, that I am the greatest flute-player in the world: and several others, of equally authoritative judgment, have given me almost equal encouragement to work with my pen. . . .

My dear father, think how for twenty years, through poverty, through pain, through weariness, through sickness, through the uncongenial atmosphere of a farcical college and of a bare army and then of an exacting business life, through all the discouragements of being wholly unacquainted with literary people and literary ways—I say, think how, in spite of all these depressing circumstances, and of a thousand more which I could enumerate, these two figures of music and poetry have steadily kept in my heart so that I could not banish them. Does it not seem to you as to me, that I begin to have a right to enroll myself among the devotees of those two sublime arts, after having followed them so long and so humbly, and through so much bitterness?

When, at last, he was able to gain an uncertain foothold in the profession of music by the award of the post of first flutist with the Peabody Orchestra, his spirits soared, although his health was still delicate and precarious. We have an account of his delight in his first experience with the orchestra in rehearsal that reflects his rich emotional involvement with the music, as well as his quaint humor. This is a portion of a letter, dated at Baltimore on December 2, 1873, and addressed to his wife, who, because of fi-

nancial stringencies, had not yet been able to join her husband in his newly adopted home. You will note the
whimsical adaptation of Elizabethan idiom, not by way of
affectation, but for affection's sake:

Well, Flauto Primo hath been to his first rehearsal.

Fancy thy poor lover, weary, worn, and stuffed with a cold,
arriving after a brisk walk—he was *so* afraid he might be behind time—at the hall of Peabody Institute. . . . Well, I sit
down, some late-comers arrive, stamping and blowing—for it
is snowing outside—and pull the green baize covers off their
big horns and bass-fiddles. Presently the Maestro, who is rush-
ing about, hither and thither, in some excitement, falleth to
striking a great tuning-fork with a mallet, and straightway we
all begin to toot A, to puff it, to groan it, to squeak it, to scrape
it, until I sympathize with the poor letter, and glide off in some
delicate little runs: and presently the others begin to flourish
also, and here we have it, up chromatics, down diatonics, un-
earthly buzzings from the big fiddles, diabolical four-string
chords from the 'cellos, passionate shrieks from the clarionets
and oboes, manly remonstrances from the horns, querulous
complaints from the bassons, and so on.

Now the Maestro mounteth to his perch. I am seated immediately next the audience, facing the first violins, who are
separated from me by the conductor's stand. I place my part,
(of the Fifth Symphony of Beethoven, which I had procured
two days before, in order to look over it, being told that on
the first rehearsal we would try nothing but the Fifth Symphony) on my stand, and try to stop my heart from beating so
fast—with unavailing arguments.

Maestro rappeth with his *baton,* and magically stilleth all
shrieks and agonies of the instruments. "Fierst" (he saith, with
the Frenchiest of French accents—tho' a Dane, he was educated in Paris), "I wish to present to ze gentlemen of ze orchestra our fierst flutist, Mr. Sidney Lanier, also our fierst oboe,
Mr." (I didn't catch his name). Whereupon, not knowing
what else to do—and the pause being somewhat awkward—I
rise and make a profound bow to the Reeds, who sit behind
me, another to the 'Celli, the Bassi, and the Tympani, in the
middle, and a third to the Violins opposite. This appeareth

to be the right thing, for Oboe jumpeth up also, and boweth, and the gentlemen of the Orchestra all rise and bow, some of them with great *empressement.* Then there is a little idiotic hum and simper, such as newly introduced people usually affect.

Then cometh a man—whom I should always hate, if I *could* hate anybody always—and, to my horror, putteth on my music-stand the flauto primo part of Niels Gade's *Ossian* Overture, and thereupon the Maestro saith, "We will try *that* fierst." Horrors! They told me they would play nothing but the Fifth Symphony, and this Ossian Overture I have never seen nor heard! This does not help my heartbeats, nor steady my lips—thou canst believe! However, there is no time to tarry, the *baton* rappeth, the horns blow, my five bars rest is out—I plunge.

Oh! If thou couldst but be by me in this sublime glory of music! All through it I yearned for thee with heart-breaking eagerness. The beauty of it maketh me catch my breath—to write of it. I will not attempt to describe it. It is the spirit of the poems of Ossian done in music by the wonderful Niels Gade. . . .

This very evident happiness in a new world of music was accompanied by an improvement in the productivity and in the quality of his poetry. Biographers and critics alike agree that the period of Lanier's best poetry dates from the year 1874.

One learns much about the character of Lanier and of his activities during the latter part of his career through the correspondence with two staunch and helpful friends, Gibson Peacock, editor of the Philadelphia *Evening Bulletin,* and Bayard Taylor, the poet.

The friendship with Peacock began in the spring of 1875 as a result of highly favorable reviews that the editor gave to Lanier's poetry, among them an especially gratifying revew of "The Symphony." Bayard Taylor was a mutual friend, and it was through the recommendation of

Peacock and Taylor that Lanier was commissioned to write
a cantata for the opening of the Centennial Exhibition at
Philadelphia in 1876. The text was given the title "Psalm
of the West." It was set to music by Dudley Buck and was
performed by a chorus of eight hundred voices with orchestra under the direction of Theodore Thomas, at that
time America's most eminent conductor. The poem, which
was published separately prior to the performance of the
cantata, attracted more notice from the public than Lanier
had yet received—not all of it favorable, owing, in part, to
a misunderstanding of the choral-orchestral nature of the
work.

Professor Starke has pointed out the fact that among the
most enthusiastic commentators upon the performance of
the cantata was President Gilman, of Johns Hopkins University, who said, "It held the attention of the vast throng
of listeners. . . . When it was concluded, loud applause
rang through the air. A noble conception had been nobly
rendered. . . . Lanier had triumphed. It was the opportunity of a lifetime to test upon a grand scale his theory of
verse. He had come off victorious" (Aubrey H. Starke,
Sidney Lanier [Chapel Hill, 1933], p. 244.)

When, in 1878, Bayard Taylor was appointed Minister
to Germany, Lanier's delight at the honor accorded his
friend was frequently mentioned in his correspondence. In
the last letter written to Taylor he addressed him jokingly,
with a quotation from *Hamlet:* "[Dear Minister]—
always a minister of grace to me—"; and later on he tells
Taylor of buying a copy of Wotton's *Reliquiae,* pretend-
ing that he did so on account of Sir Henry's punning
definition of an ambassador, which Lanier changes to
"minister" in Taylor's honor.

A short time ago I found in a second-hand bookstall a copy of Sir Henry Wotton's works and letters printed in 1685, and bought it—with about all the money I had; for a joke of old Sir Henry's on a minister carried my mind to you. Having been asked, (he narrates the story himself, being then on a ministerial journey through Germany) to write in an album, he chose to define a minister, and said: *A Minister is a man sent to lie abroad for the good of his country.*

Farther along in the same letter he tells Taylor of an experiment with dactyls in a poem called "The Revenge of Hamish"; and he forecasts the publication of another freer treatment of the same rhythm in a poem which he is going to call "The Marshes of Glynn." He has hopes of finding a publisher for *The Science of English Verse;* and, as though this did not reflect activity enough, he speaks of a contract with Scribner's for a "Boy's Froissart," and of wishing to publish an historical account, in two volumes, of *The English Sonnet-Makers from Surrey to Shakespeare.*

I shall refer to Lanier's technical treatise on prosody, *The Science of English Verse,* mainly to note the following points:

First, that it was the only book based upon his Shakespeare lectures that was published during his lifetime. He saw it through the press in May, 1880, only a little more than a year before his death, and therefore a pathetically short time after he had commenced the series of university lectures to which he had looked forward so eagerly.

Second, that the genesis of the book has been traced by Professor Paul F. Baum in his Introduction to Volume II of the Centennial Edition of Lanier's *Works.* He notes three stages, beginning with a group of articles called "The Physics of Poetry," written for *Lippincott's Maga-*

zine in the summer of 1878. These, in turn, were based upon material given in a series of informal Shakespeare lectures in Baltimore during the previous spring. This fact helps to explain the prominence of Shakespeare quotation in the book, as well as numerous citations from minor Elizabethans. The third strand of the three-fold source consists of material prepared for his Johns Hopkins lectures which were yet to be delivered, although Lanier must certainly have rewritten a good deal of this for the lectures proper.

I note, finally, on the point of composition and structure, that the completion of the book was hurried because of his hopes for more extensive teaching opportunities in new courses in the University; and the work contains certain blemishes that are quite evidently the result of haste.

While, as I have indicated, there were some external reasons for the frequency of Shakespearean quotation and illustration in *The Science of English Verse,* I am persuaded that it was his appreciation of the range and catholicity of Shakespeare's language and of its poetic flexibility that Lanier found irresistible for his purposes. This may be illustrated by the following extract, which is all that I shall take time to quote from that rather technical and controversial treatise. In Part I, Chapter V, which deals with rhythm, he has this to say about Shakespeare's use of rhythmic accent:

In his peculiar management of the rhythmic accent . . . Shakspere's supreme mastery of the technic of blank verse shows itself with great clearness. We can see him learning to think in verse. Indeed, growing always, in the way of the artist—always profiting by the practice of his earlier comedy, or his middle-period tragedy—always converting acquisition into second nature—he finally made his whole technic a constitutional grace, so that his passion flowed with a hereditary pre-adaptation to rhythm.

The great underlying principle, however, of all Shakspere's applications of his technic in practise was a superb confidence in the common rhythmic perception of men and a clear insight into the rhythmic habit of familiar English utterance.

This method of working with a constant inward reference to the great average and sum of men, and with an absolute reliance upon their final perception, is the secret of that infinitely-varied rhythm which we find plashing through all the later verse of Shakspere. . . .

Perhaps every one has observed that particularly in Shakspere's later plays he seems absolutely careless as to what kind of word the rhythmic accent may fall on. Sometimes it is the article *the,* sometimes the preposition *of,* sometimes the conjunction *and.* . . .

This apparent carelessness is really perfect art. It is the consummate management of dramatic dialogue in blank verse, by which the wilder rhythmic patterns of ordinary current discourse are woven along through the regular strands of the orderly typic lines. [*The Centennial Edition of the Works of Sidney Lanier* (Baltimore: The Johns Hopkins Press, 1945), II, 166–167.]

In order to avoid giving the impression that Lanier was mainly engaged with questions of technique, let me indicate his treatment of a familiar passage from *The Merchant of Venice.*

The opening scene of Act V is set in the gardens before Portia's house at Belmont. Here Lorenzo, enchanted by the magic of the moonlight and of Jessica's presence, and loath to go inside, begins his speech with the well-remembered lines:

> How sweet the moonlight sleeps upon this bank!
> Here will we sit and let the sounds of music
> Creep in our ears. Soft stillness and the night

> Become the touches of sweet harmony.
> Sit, Jessica. Look how the floor of heaven
> Is thick-inlaid with patens of bright gold.

[And so on]

The "and so on" consists of a lecture that runs for thirty-five more lines—a treatise on the "sweet power of music," complete with Ovidian mythological allusion, and concluded with the familiar condemnation of that untrustworthy, unmusical man who is fit for "treasons, stratagems, and spoils."

Midway of Lorenzo's discourse, an opening is afforded Jessica when the background music has begun, and she makes one of those luminous, utterly simple, one-sentence statements which are part of the wonder of Shakespeare. She says,

> I am never merry when I hear sweet music.

Lanier's comment is to be found in his *Shakspere and His Forerunners* (Vol. II, p. 23):

Jessica here pierces quite near to the root of the matter, namely, to that infinite underfeeling of serious and illimitable desire which every one who *knows* music understands and which *no* one who knows music will attempt to describe. It seems much that any hint of this should have dawned upon Shakspere, when we reflect that he died, poor soul! seventy years before Bach was born, a hundred and fifty-odd years before Beethoven was born; that he knew nothing of the orchestra; that, in short, he never heard anything that we would call great music.

[Lanier notes further] The sharp contrast between the feeling here expressed by Jessica and the primitive conception of music is strikingly shown by the derivation of our word *glee,* meaning joy, or mirth, from the Anglo-Saxon gliȝ, which meant music or song. Jessica's remark is the first note we hear of the modern sorrow-cultus in music.

When, in July, 1879, Lanier wrote to President Gilman in connection with his own appointment as lecturer in the Johns Hopkins University, he was concerned to distinguish between the two series of lectures that he was expected to give. He enclosed an outline of his proposed program, calling attention to an ambitious list of typical theses (seven of them) on which the advanced students in the university would be expected to work.

"I wish," he writes, "to get some young Americans at hard work in pure literature, and will be glad if the public lectures in Hopkins Hall shall be merely accessory to my main course." Lanier then points out the main features of his thesis plan, which bears some marked resemblances to what are often called programs of independent study, or honors courses, in our colleges today. He emphasizes particularly the following points:

(1) Each of the programs involves original research, and will—if properly carried out—constitute a genuine contribution to modern literary scholarship;

(2) Each is so arranged as to fall in with various other studies and extend their range—for example, the first one being suitable to a student of philology who is pursuing Anglo-Saxon; [the 2nd] to one who is studying the transition period of English; [another] to one who is studying Elizabethan English, and so on;

(3) Each project necessitates diligent study of some great English work, not as a philological collection of words, but as pure literature; and the general principle that

(4) They all keep steadily in view, as their ultimate object, that strengthening of manhood, that enlarging of sympathy, that glorifying of moral purpose, which the student unconsciously gains, not from direct didacti-

cism, but from this constant association with our finest ideals and loftiest souls.

In advocacy of his broad view of literary studies, Lanier makes a comment that has a distinctly modern ring, and might indeed have been written by one of our contemporary humanists interested in achieving a better balance among our curricular offerings, or perhaps by a proponent of the establishment of a National Humanities Foundation along the lines of the National Science Foundation. Still addressing President Gilman, Lanier writes: "I think I can already perceive a certain narrowness of sympathy and—what is worse—an unsymmetric development of faculty both intellectual and moral, from a too-exclusive devotion to Science, which Science itself would be the first to condemn."

Although the University could not accommodate Lanier with as ambitious a program as he had hoped for, he gained at least the appointment as lecturer and plunged into a busy regimen of reading and review by way of preparation for the series of lectures. His enjoyment of the task is indicated in a letter to Taylor, written on October 20:

Indeed I have been so buried in study for the past six months that I know not news nor gossip of any kind. Such days and nights of glory as I have had! [In the Peabody Library] I have been studying Early English, Middle English, and Elizabethan English . . . and the world seems twice as large.

A little later Lanier broached an idea to Gibson Peacock that is significant for its originality and for its prophecy; for in it he sowed the seeds which later sprang up in the Johns Hopkins and other universities and bore fruit in the establishment of programs in what we now call adult education:

167

This stage of the investigation put me to thinking of schools for grown people. Men and women leave college nowadays just at the time when they are really prepared to study with effect, . . . to pursue some regular course of thought: but there is no guidance, no organized means of any sort, by which people engaged in ordinary avocations can accomplish such an aim.

After presenting some additional arguments, Lanier concludes, "In short, the present miscellaneous lecture courses ought to die and be born again as *Schools for Grown People.*" Among others to whom Lanier submitted this proposal was Horace Howard Furness, who expressed a kindly interest but could give no encouragement at the time. Many years had to pass before the movement which Lanier foresaw could gain its full momentum.

Meanwhile he threw himself with all the fervor that his health would permit into his Shakespeare lectures, his own poetry, and into other plans for extending his academic offerings whenever the hoped-for opportunity should come.

His Shakespeare course of sixteen lectures began, as we have seen, in the fall term of the academic year 1879–1880. While the lectures were open to the public, as President Gilman wished, they were yet a part of the regular university curriculum and were remarkably well attended, the average number of listeners being 170. In addition, Lanier gave two courses restricted to advanced students in the University, the first dealing with certain poems of Chaucer and with Shakespeare's *A Midsummer Night's Dream, Hamlet,* and *The Tempest.* The other course, which, interestingly enough, was limited to students of science, was called the Art of Expression. The substance of these latter lectures, under the title, "Chaucer and Shakespeare," has been published separately in Volume IV of the Centennial Edition.

Because of serious and almost continuous illness, he was restricted in the following (and last) year of his teaching to only one course—that on the English Novel. Another course on Shakespeare was announced for the fall of 1881, but the characteristic hopefulness with which he assumed this obligation was finally defeated, and he died on September 7.

Many years after Lanier's death the bulk of the lectures were published under the supervision of the poet's son, Henry W. Lanier, with the title *Shakspere and His Forerunners*. The work was handsomely printed in two volumes in New York in 1902 and the following year in London. Except for a brief preface, no attempt was made to provide the text with editorial apparatus, and it was stated that the "editorial work has consisted entirely of selection and arrangement," with "merely a little pruning of repetitions and of matters elaborated in *The Science of Verse*."

Forty-three years later, upon the publication of the Centennial Edition of Lanier's *Works* by the Johns Hopkins University Press, the material contained in the 1902 edition was re-examined and compared with the manuscripts, which by now were in the University collections; and a different plan of presentation was adopted. This plan is lucidly explained in the excellent Editorial Introduction to Volume III, provided by Professor Kemp Malone. It was he who, in addition to performing customary editorial duties, undertook the involved and trying task of analysis and reorganization, in order to make available a useful and scholarly text.

Frederick Hard

Professor Malone's critical comments upon the lectures are both discriminating and generous. In suggesting the treatment of certain errors in the lectures, he distinguishes between "mistakes that are personal to the author and those which reflect the state of scholarship in the author's day." As an example of the latter he cites the lectures on English pronunciation as reflective of the monumental, but now outdated, work of A. J. Ellis; and naturally, he says, the lectures "echo the errors of their source." He adds that fortunately only a few pages are affected by these errors, and even here only in part, "since Ellis was right about many points." The other type of error, into which Lanier was sometimes led by his "speculative connections," is occasionally too fanciful for serious treatment. "More often, however," continues the editor, "Lanier's combinations and comparisons, insights of a fertile and imaginative genius, prove valuable: suggestive, provocative, sometimes brilliant and illuminating." In a concluding statement Professor Malone refers the reader to the last group of lectures "with the assurance that he will find them learned, interesting, and characteristic both of Lanier and of his time."

It would be hard to imagine two literary figures more different in talent, temperament, and temper than Sidney Lanier and George Bernard Shaw. Yet they had one quality in common, namely, an almost passionate regard for the music of Shakespeare's words, and a rich understanding of its significance for a full appreciation of the plays.

Because of Shaw's phenomenally long life we are apt not to realize that, at the time of Lanier's death in 1881, Shaw was already established as a critic of music. But it is true that throughout his long and tempestuous career he never lost sight of the importance of that art, both on its own account and because of its relations to literature.

One finds in each of these writers, who are otherwise in such contrast as to background, upbringing, and outlook, a very similar sensitivity to the tone, timbre, and overtones of Shakespeare's expressive language, the knowledge of which can add much to one's enjoyment of the subtler nuances of Shakespeare's art.

Needless to say, the language and tone of Shaw's critical declamations—usually in the form of witty aspersions upon the style of a bombastic actor or a clumsy manager—are quite different in manner and manners from those of Lanier. It may be entertaining to cite a few of Shaw's incisive comments on the music of Shakespeare's plays, most of what I shall choose having been written in connection with his function as critic, not of music, but of drama, and hence, perhaps, all the more relevant.

But before doing that I should like to review with you the question as to what Shaw really thought of Shakespeare.

In the latest edition of his biography of Shaw, Archibald Henderson has a chapter called "Blaming the Bard," which gives a shrewd and lively account of the matter, with the conclusion that, in spite of all his impudencies, caustic exaggerations, impieties, and injustices, Shaw nevertheless rendered "an indispensable service to literature and public opinion."

Granting for the moment that Shaw was motivated by a concern for the public interest, it is certain that in order to qualify for the task of iconoclast he himself had to know

Shakespeare very thoroughly. And I think we can take his word for it that he did. On one occasion, writing for the *Saturday Review,* he said that Shakespeare

has outlasted thousands of abler thinkers and will outlast a thousand more. His gift of telling a story (provided some one else told it to him first); his enormous power over language, as conspicuous in his senseless and silly abuse of it as in his miracles of expression; his humor; his sense of idiosyncratic character; and his prodigious fund of that vital energy which is, it seems, the true differentiating property behind the faculties, good, bad, or indifferent, of the man of genius, enable him to entertain us so effectively that the imaginary scenes and people he has created become more real to us than our actual life. . . . When I was twenty I knew everybody in Shakespeare, from Hamlet to Abhorson, much more intimately than I knew my living contemporaries.

Henderson also quotes Shaw, at the conclusion of the chapter that I have already referred to, as saying, sagely, "When I began to write, William was a divinity and a bore. Now he is a fellow-creature." Henderson notes further that Shaw's criticism of Shakespeare promised to give rise to a wealth of analysis and commentary. Thus far, he said, "surprisingly little has been written on the subject." I believe that this defect has now been partly remedied by the recent publication of Edwin Wilson's book *Shaw on Shakespeare,* which is prefaced by an amusing and suggestive essay. This anthology includes the comment quoted above and the three or four which I shall now quote. They are representative, I think, of what we may call his musical view of Shakespeare. He says, first, "The ear is the sure clue" to Shakespeare; "only a musician can understand the play of feeling which is the real rarity in his early plays. In a deaf nation these plays would have died long ago."

Again, he says, "Comparatively few of Shakespeare's admirers are at all conscious that they are listening to music as they hear his phrases turn and his lines fall so fascinatingly and memorably."

Turning to analogy, Shaw declares, "It is the score and not the libretto that keeps the work alive and fresh; and this is why only musical critics should be allowed to meddle with Shakespeare."

Grouping four of Shakespeare's plays together, Shaw says firmly:

The two Richards, King John, and the last act of *Romeo and Juliet* depend wholly on the beauty of their music. There is no deep significance, no great subtlety and variety in their numbers; but, for splendor of sound, magic of romantic illusion, majesty of emphasis, ardor, elation, reverberation of haunting echoes, and every poetic quality that can waken the heart-stir and the imaginative fire of early manhood, they stand above all recorded music. These things cannot be spectated . . . ; they must be heard.

Notwithstanding such praise of Shakespeare and his considered judgment that "In manner and art nobody can write better," Shaw bases his real, or pretended, quarrel with Shakespeare's reputation on the ground that a dramatist should always be preoccupied with contemporary political, religious, and moral problems and "the bearing of these on communities, which is sociology." In effect, Shaw blames Shakespeare for not being Ibsen; although he makes oblique confessions of his paradoxical prejudices, he insists officially that Shakespeare's great defect was a want of social philosophy, and he harps continuously upon that string.

In contrast, Sidney Lanier leaves no doubt about his

faith in Shakespeare as a moral teacher; and I am afraid that Shaw would have regarded him as a confirmed Bardolater. By no stretch could Lanier have made the convenient separation between the meaning and the music, as Shaw affects to do, or to distinguish so arbitrarily between the "manner of art" and the "matter." To him, the music, the magic, and the message were all one.

Lanier's favorite theme, in poetry, in music, and in drama is that of the resolution of discords; and in life, the resolution of antagonisms. In the thirteenth of the Johns Hopkins lectures, after a careful comparison of the verse characteristics of Shakespeare's early and later plays with their contrasts and variations, he declares:

> In short, Shakspere's general advance is clearly a more *artistic balancing of the oppositions which constitute verse;* and this idea enables us now to present a perfectly clear statement of that artistic advance in terms of our theory of oppositions, and thus to bring out this artistic advance as only one side of his general moral advance.

And further along, he says:

> Let us take the *Midsummer Night's Dream,* which we can prove by all sorts of evidence, positive, indirect, external, internal, metrical tests, higher tests, and all, to represent Shakspere's first period, and let us contrast this with *The Tempest,* which we can prove nearly as conclusively to represent his last period. . . . In both we have man's relation towards nature— nature tricksy in the Puck and Oberon of the one, nature conquered and drawing water for man in the allayed tempest and the monster servant Caliban of the other; again, the *Midsummer Night's Dream* shows us man's relations to man in the twist and cross of love which never runs smooth, . . . while *The Tempest* shows us the same relations to one's fellow-men in the affairs of power, of ambition, of state, of fatherhood, of love, of forgiveness, and so on. And, to make their fitness for comparison grow to the exquisite degree, both these plays are

a sort of fairytales, admitting unbounded freedom of treatment and unshackled by any such considerations of time or place or environment as would prevent Shakspere from giving his full and untrammelled utterance.

Following a discussion of the great tragedies and the "bitter" comedies in Lecture XII, he wrote:

Instead of the bleak storms of the *Hamlet* and *Macbeth* time, now we have the great and beautiful calm of a spirit which, after having seen and shared in all the crime and all the grief in the world, has at length attained God out of knowledge and good out of infinite pain. If you contemplate this group of plays which I have here placed in the last period, you find them all hinging upon the sweet that follows the bitter: *Pericles, Cymbeline, Tempest, Winter's Tale, Henry VIII,* all these, in great and noble music, breathe of new love after estrangement, of the recovery of long-lost children, of the kissing of wives thought dead, of reconciliation, of new births of old happiness—most of all, of sweeping magnanimity, of heavenly forgiveness.

Again Lanier, by way of considering what the poet's noblest function may be, carries forward this discussion, elevating it to a high pitch in the conclusion of the lecture which follows the one I have just quoted:

We may recognise that supreme value of the poet . . . who balances these terrible oppositions of life, balances them, not in ignorance, not by shutting his eyes upon them, but by that enormous faith which, seeing them, is not dismayed. It is he, the poet, who moves with level eye down this lane of life hedged about with these mysteries, and keeps Love and Reconciliation alive with art and music. It is our Shakspere who, . . . using his art to allay tempests and to bring all things right and to set forth Prospero's prodigious forgiveness of his brother's injury—it is our Shakspere who then makes us cry, amid the heart-breaking perplexities of life's oppositions and complex antagonisms, *Sursum corda! Here is a poet who met these oppositions and managed them; and do but listen to our Shakspere singing in the dark!*

I am going to close, as Lanier sometimes closed his own lectures, on a sentimental note. On one particular occasion, in speaking of Shakespeare's latter days, after he had left London for Stratford to rejoin his wife and family, from whom he had absented himself so long, Lanier said to the members of his class:

I take great pleasure in contemplating what seems to be the only genuine relic of Shakspere preserved at Stratford, and which brings vividly to our eyes this period of peaceful reunion with his wife and of tranquil life in the tranquil Warwick country. The relic I speak of is a round piece of glass some four or five inches in diameter on which are painted the letters W and A—for *William* and *Anne*—under the common letter S for *Shakespeare,* with the date 1615, as if it were a sort of memorial of the enclosure of the life of this once parted William and Anne in a final circle of harmony, reconciliation, and pardon.

It so happens that this "relic" is among the association items now housed in the Folger Shakespeare Library.

Whatever may be our final view of the importance of Lanier's contribution to learning, we can, I believe, agree that he was a complete gentleman, a richly gifted poet and musician, a sensitive and constructive critic, and an original, stimulating, and dedicated teacher. That he should have died at the age of thirty-nine, with little chance of fulfilling the potentialities that were so promising, is a sad reflection. But I think he deserves to be remembered today, and in this place, for his enthusiastic, imaginative, and steadfast love for the poems and plays of William Shakespeare.